AF426449

The Shoot of Jesse

A Savior Promised through the Jesse Tree

R.A. Sweeney

Artwork by

Sydney C.G. Wallace

REMEMBER YOUR TREE ORNAMENTS

The artwork from the book has matching ornaments!
Go to www.davekbooks.com/about-the-book
to get your ornaments to accompany the book.

THE SHOOT OF JESSE

R.A. SWEENEY

R.A. SWEENEY

The Hope from Jesse

The story of the Old Testament tells of the search for a leader for God's people. God had designed all creation to function under the rule of a royal priest in league with God, reigning from God's garden paradise. Throughout the story, kings, prophets, and priests all rose and fell. Each one was flawed and failed to be completely obedient to God and lead others in that same obedience. The closest the story ever came was David. Even though David failed again and again, he loved God with his entire heart, sought to obey Him, and led others in obedience better than anyone else.

But after David died, his descendants failed to follow his example. Even the best of them were mere shadows. Because of their unfaithfulness and unrighteousness, God spoke through the prophet Isaiah that He would chop down the tree that represented David's family line. It would be taken down to the roots and burned for good measure. Their wickedness could not be allowed to grow any longer. Creation needed a new hope, and someone from David's line was not the answer because we had seen how David's descendants had failed.

God also spoke another message through Isaiah. He foretold that even though the line of David had been cut down to a stump and burned, a new *shoot* would arise from the root of Jesse, David's father, and grow into a *tree of life*. This new shoot would bring God's blessing to all parts of creation and set all things right. This shoot was described as a ruler who would reign with righteousness and mercy for all eternity. The promise was not that God would raise up

THE SHOOT OF JESSE

someone who took after David, as his sons did. The promise was to raise up a new and better David.

Each day, you will read a part of the story leading up to this prophetic pronouncement and then following the prophecy to its completion. Read each story. Reflect on the Scripture. Then, hang the accompanying ornament on your tree. By the end, your tree will tell the story of the promised Shoot from the line of Jesse, who grew to become our Tree of Life.

Then a shoot will spring from the stem of Jesse,

And a branch from his roots will bear fruit.

The Spirit of the LORD will rest on Him,

The spirit of wisdom and understanding,

The spirit of counsel and strength,

The spirit of knowledge and the fear of the LORD.

And He will delight in the fear of the LORD,

And He will not judge by what His eyes see,

Nor make a decision by what His ears hear;

But with righteousness He will judge the poor,

And decide with fairness for the afflicted of the earth;

And He will strike the earth with the rod of His mouth,

And with the breath of His lips He will slay the wicked.

Also righteousness will be the belt about His loins,

And faithfulness the belt about His waist.

~ ISAIAH 11:1–5

THE SHOOT OF JESSE

December 1
CREATION

The Bible begins with two distinct stories of creation. These are not the only depictions of creation in the Bible, but they are the primary pictures God gives us to help us understand creation. The Bible begins with the words, "In the beginning, God created the Heavens and the Earth."[1]

The Hebrew word for "in the beginning" does not mean the first thing that ever happened but the beginning of the story that is about to be told. I am reminded of the movie, *The Hobbit*, which begins with, "It began long ago, in a land far away to the east."[2] If you know Tolkien's work, you know that the universe of this story had existed for thousands of years before these events, but the story started by introducing its beginning with "It began." This is how the Bible starts. While there is nothing to say these aren't the first events that ever happened, the story itself doesn't make that claim.

The other important detail is what it means that God created the universe. The Hebrew word for *created* literally means "ordered" or "established purpose." The story of creation is the story of God ordering the cosmos. This fits because the cosmos is originally described as uninhabitable and uninhabited.[3] The world was a place where life could not thrive, and so it didn't. God then spent three days structuring the cosmos. He made time, seas, skies, dry land, and plants. Then He spent three days populating the cosmos. He made spiritual beings to inhabit the heavens, birds to populate the skies, sea creatures to populate the waters, and land creatures to populate the land.

This is a common story in the ancient Middle East. Many of the religions from that time and place had creation narratives similar to this. The story of a god ordering the cosmos in six days is how they would talk about the building of a *temple space*. The temple spaces were the divine control rooms of the universe. It was usually a beautiful garden from where the god would rule the universe.

So, when God put something in the middle of the garden temple, you expect it to be an idol statue. In fact, He called the thing He put in the middle His *image*, which is the same Hebrew word often used to describe idol statues. But here, the idol in the garden temple is a human. In ancient Near Eastern culture, idol statues were believed to be the physical manifestation on the earth of the god they represented. This made humans the means through which God interacted with the physical world. They were God's connection point with the world.

In the second narrative of creation, we see the same picture. Humans were sculpted like statues and placed in the garden to cultivate the garden. Once the humans were placed there, the plants and animals began to thrive. The river began to flow out of the garden as well, and brought life to the rest of the world. In this version of the story, having a human in the temple was the way God's blessings came to the earth and were spread to all the land.

In Genesis chapter 1, the humans were told to fill the earth and rule over it. In chapter 2, they were told to tend (take care of) the garden. Between the two pictures, we can see that humans were made to rule, like kings, and work in the temple, like priests. Humans were to be royal priests as God's representatives on the earth in order to bring God's blessings to all creation.

The universe is meant to operate with a royal priest, working in partnership with God. This is how the world can receive God's blessing. This is how the machine was made to run. Without these types of humans, the universe cannot operate correctly.

THE SHOOT OF JESSE

Then God said, "Let Us make man in Our image, according to Our likeness; and let them rule over the fish of the sea and over the birds of the sky and over the cattle and over all the earth, and over every creeping thing that creeps on the earth." God created man in His own image, in the image of God He created him; male and female He created them. God blessed them; and God said to them, "Be fruitful and multiply, and fill the earth, and subdue it; and rule over the fish of the sea and over the birds of the sky and over every living thing that moves on the earth." . . .

R.A. SWEENEY

Then God said, "Behold, I have given you every plant yielding seed that is on the surface of all the earth, and every tree which has fruit yielding seed; it shall be food for you; and to every beast of the earth and to every bird of the sky and to every thing that moves on the earth which has life, I have given every green plant for food"; and it was so. God saw all that He had made, and behold, it was very good. And there was evening and there was morning, the sixth day.

~ GENESIS 1:26–31

THE SHOOT OF JESSE

December 2
THE SIN SERPENT

The man and woman lived in the garden and had unlimited, unhindered access to God. God gave them the freedom to enjoy the entire garden. He put trees there that were pretty. He put trees there that smelled wonderful. He put trees there that produced fruit. He even planted a tree in the middle that provided a way for humans to interact with God. But He also planted one single tree in the garden that represented the ability to choose for yourself how to rule the world. God put this tree there to give the humans the choice to obey or rebel, but He told them that if they ate from this tree, they would be cut off from the life He offers.

One day, something called a *Serpent* interacted with the woman. The Serpent was described as a beast of the wilderness, but it was in the garden for some reason—it had crossed over from its designated space into somewhere it did not belong. This Serpent was also described using language that implied it was another type of creature going somewhere it didn't belong—a spiritual being.

The Serpent tricked the humans into eating from the one tree they were forbidden to eat from. Immediately, the man and woman began to feel the effects. Their relationship with God was damaged, as was their relationship with each other. When God confronted them about it, He gave them a chance to repent. Rather than repenting, they blamed each other and blamed God.

As a result, God pronounced the consequences of

their actions. Relationships between humans were fundamentally broken. Relationships with God were severed. The ground and animals would not function as they were meant to. The spiritual being was banished from the heavens and bound to the earth. The relationship between the humans and the spiritual beings became oppositional. All the order that God had created was impacted once the royal priests had abandoned their vocation and abandoned the God they were supposed to represent. God designed the universe to function with human royal priests working in partnership with Him. So, when that partnership fell apart, the world began to come off the rails.

Outside Eden, the man and woman had children. The two oldest, Cain and Abel, both came to the door of the garden with sacrifices, trying to fix the ruin of their parents. God looked favorably upon Abel's sacrifice but did not look favorably on Cain's. This made Cain upset. God came to Cain to give him wisdom, instruction, and warning. He told Cain that He was still generous and would provide abundantly to everyone who did what was good. He warned Cain, though, that if he did not do well, something called *Sin* was crouching, like a wild beast, desiring to devour him. God reminded Cain that he was made to be a king over all creation, including this snakey thing called Sin.

Cain proved to be like his parents. The Sin Serpent deceived him. He took his brother, Abel, the one who had found favor in God's eyes, into the wilderness. Out there, the Sin Serpent devoured Cain by deceiving him into killing his brother.

Again, God gave Cain the chance to repent. Cain,

instead, rejected God's provision and built a city to provide for himself and protect himself. This was the start of the Serpent's kingdom. Seven generations in, this kingdom was producing arts, engineering, and science. It was a new paradise, but without God—an imitation of Eden—but distorted. While the kingdom was advancing, corruption was progressing too. Men were claiming women as property (an amplification of one of the consequences God pronounced to Adam and Eve) and were killing indiscriminately (an amplification of the sin of Cain).

The Sin Serpent had enslaved humanity and was establishing its own kingdom to rival Eden.

THE SHOOT OF JESSE

*So the L*ᴏʀᴅ *God said to the serpent, "Because*
you have done this,

"Cursed are you above all livestock
and all wild animals!
You will crawl on your belly
and you will eat dust
all the days of your life.
And I will put enmity
between you and the woman,
and between your offspring and hers;
he will crush your head,
and you will strike his heel."

~ Gᴇɴᴇsɪs 3:14–15 NIV

R.A. SWEENEY

Therefore the LORD *God sent him out from the garden of Eden, to cultivate the ground from which he was taken. So He drove the man out; and at the east of the garden of Eden He stationed the cherubim and the flaming sword which turned every direction to guard the way to the tree of life.*

~ GENESIS 3:23–24

Then the LORD *said to Cain, "Why are you angry? And why has your countenance fallen? If you do well, will not your countenance be lifted up? And if you do not do well, sin is crouching at the door; and its desire is for you, but you must master it."*

~ GENESIS 4:6–7

THE SHOOT OF JESSE

December 3
BREAKING POINT

While Cain's family grew to create the kingdom of the Serpent, Adam and Eve had another son, Seth, who was also starting a family. But Seth's family kept dying. They were a people who called on the name of God, but they still lived outside of Eden and were separated from the life God originally wanted for His people.

The world became worse and worse from generation to generation. Humans and spiritual beings continued to cross boundaries and work with each other in rebellion against God. The kingdom of the Serpent was destroying the goodness of the world by spreading violence and injustice. God's passion for His creation finally drove Him to act. He needed to act against the rebellious parts of His creation to stop their destruction of the rest of creation.

One man found favor in God's sight, Noah. God instructed Noah to create a giant wooden box, which we translate as ark, to be filled with seeds for a new garden of Eden. It was a miniature floating Eden box. God had Noah and his family enter the box, and He sent every type of animal He wanted to preserve into the box as well. Then, God closed the door to the box and began His work. God removed the boundaries of the seas that He had established on day three of the Genesis 1 account of creation and removed the sky that held back the waters of the heavens that He had established on day two. He undid creation and allowed the cosmos to collapse back in upon itself. Every part of creation was destroyed except this single floating

Eden seed. God reestablished the order from days two and three and planted the wooden-box-seed on a high mountain to make a new Eden. Noah and his family planted a garden. They tended the animals as their rulers, and Noah even built an altar to offer sacrifices, like a priest. A new Eden had been made with a new royal priest serving God.

But this Eden did not last long. Noah fell into sin, along with his son. The Serpent's kingdom had been destroyed, but the Serpent was still alive. A new generation of humans had become enslaved by the Serpent.

The family of Noah grew. His three sons had sons, and those sons had sons. They spread out throughout the region until one of the sons rose up as a leader. Nimrod was a powerful man. He was a mighty slayer of both man and beast. He began creating cities, just like Cain. The chief city was called Babylon. Here, the people began inventing technology, just like in Cain's city, and they invented brickmaking. They put the technology of making bricks to use by building a tower, called a *ziggurat*. These ziggurats were pyramid-like buildings often used as palaces for royalty and would have a temple at the very top. Nimrod and the people of Babylon were going to build a ziggurat that reached so high the temple at the top would be all the way in the heavens (the place where the spiritual beings lived and beyond the boundary for humans). All the family of Noah came together as one people to make their own Eden in the heavens as a rival to God and His temple.

Once again, God saw that the wickedness of humans was going to destroy the creation He had made. He was forced to act in order to protect the creation that He loved.

R.A. SWEENEY

God changed their languages and their ideas so that they were not all one big people group but many people with different ideas, desires, and languages. This scattered the people across the world.

As the Sin Serpent continued to tighten its grasp on humanity, God kept intervening to limit its power. But humanity kept failing to turn away from the Serpent and unite with God in any lasting way. They couldn't, because the Sin Serpent enslaved them. But God would not resort to slavery to have unity with His people. Love was the only bond He would have with His people.

THE SHOOT OF JESSE

*Then the L*ORD *saw that the wickedness of man was great on the earth, and that every intent of the thoughts of his heart was only evil continually. The L*ORD *was sorry that He had made man on the earth, and He was grieved in His heart. The L*ORD *said, "I will blot out man whom I have created from the face of the land, from man to animals to creeping things and to birds of the sky; for I am sorry that I have made them." But Noah found favor in the eyes of the L*ORD *.*

*~ G*ENESIS *6:5–8*

*Then Noah built an altar to the LORD , and took
of every clean animal and of every clean bird and
offered burnt offerings on the altar. The LORD
smelled the soothing aroma; and the LORD said
to Himself, "I will never again curse the ground
on account of man, for the intent of man's heart
is evil from his youth; and I will never again
destroy every living thing, as I have done.*
"While the earth remains,
Seedtime and harvest,
And cold and heat,
And summer and winter,
And day and night
Shall not cease."

~ GENESIS 8:20–22

*They said, "Come, let us build for ourselves a city,
and a tower whose top will reach into heaven,
and let us make for ourselves a name, otherwise
we will be scattered abroad over the face of the
whole earth."*

~ GENESIS 11:4

THE SHOOT OF JESSE

December 4
FAITH CREDITED AS RIGHTEOUSNESS

As the people dispersed from Babylon when God scattered them by changing their language, He selected one family to be the family through whom He would continue His mission to rescue creation from the Sin Serpent. God called Abram, whom He later renamed Abraham, to leave behind everything he knew and everything he had in order to follow where God would lead. God promised Abraham a land that was full of abundance. He promised to give Abraham an innumerably large family. He promised to give Abraham the blessings of Eden—to be fruitful and multiply, to fill the earth and subdue it, and for all the nations of the earth to be blessed through His family. Somehow, Abraham's family was going to be the people to reenter Eden and take the role as God's image-bearing royal priests so that the cosmos could be put right again.

These were huge promises. And these promises were given without Abraham doing anything to earn them. They were purely gifts of God's generosity—the same generosity God had shown to Adam and Cain but neither had trusted. The Bible tells us that God considered Abraham to be righteous solely because Abraham trusted that God is faithful and generous[4]—meaning that God considered Abraham to have nothing that would damage their relationship. This trust put Abraham in a right relationship with God.

THE SHOOT OF JESSE

But simple trust of a promise did not qualify Abraham to reenter Eden. Abraham had many moments where he completely trusted and submitted to God. He had moments where he questioned God in order to trust Him more. He also had moments where he failed to trust God, and his actions caused brokenness and hardship for himself and everyone around him. Abraham trusted God, but he failed to live based on that trust about as often as he succeeded in putting that trust into action.

Abraham's biggest desire was to have a child. God had promised to give him many children, but Abraham became impatient. Abraham had followed in the footsteps of Eve in the garden. He decided to take what he wanted for himself rather than trusting in God's plan and timing. Abraham did have sons but not by following God's methods. This failure, like his other failures, hurt everyone around him. In the end, he had to surrender both sons into God's hands.

The son that God did give him was his second son, Isaac. When Isaac was becoming a young man, God gave Abraham a final test. God told Abraham, as a test of Abraham's ability to surrender his will and trust in God's plan, that Abraham needed to take Isaac up on a high mountain and offer him to God as a burnt sacrifice. God required Abraham to give up that which he held most dear, that which he had committed his worst sins to acquire. Abraham did not flinch. In faith, Abraham packed his bags and took his son to the mountain. In faith, they climbed up the mountain and built an altar. In faith, Abraham bound his son, placed him on the altar, and raised the knife to kill

Isaac.

The book of Hebrews tells us that Abraham trusted God's promise that Isaac would have many descendants and considered that God could raise people even from the dead[5]. In this faith, Abraham was prepared to trust God, even through death. Isaac was Abraham's pride and joy. He was Abraham's delight. But Isaac was also Abraham's life. Isaac was the way in which Abraham's life would continue after Abraham's body failed and he died. In this act of sacrifice, Abraham trusted all of God's promises enough to send his son's life, and his own, into the grave. He knew God was more powerful and generous than the grave could hold back. He entered into death in trust.

At the last moment, an angel appeared and stopped Abraham from killing Isaac. Abraham's obedient heart, obedient to the point of entering the jaws of death itself, was the sacrifice God truly required. God provided a ram for Abraham to offer in Isaac's place. Abraham and Isaac worshiped God on this mountain, which would later be the mountain upon which the city of Jerusalem would be built. Abraham had passed the test, and God told him that because of his obedience, the blessings of Eden would finally be his.

In fact, the story of Abraham's sacrifice of Isaac is bookended by stories of Abraham living the life of Eden. We are told that his family lived in a very dry region without water. But everywhere Abraham dug a well they found water. His neighbors began claiming his wells as their own—essentially stealing his wells—because they did not have enough water for themselves. Rather than getting angry

THE SHOOT OF JESSE

or fighting them, Abraham made an agreement with the neighboring king that they could have his wells. Then, Abraham hosted a big party for them all. He even provided a bunch of food from his own flock.

Immediately after the sacrifice of Isaac story, Abraham was again making treaties and agreements with the neighboring gentiles. Again, Abraham was generous and blessed his neighbors because he trusted he had enough. Abraham had abundance wherever he went. He came to trust God's generosity so much that everyone else around him received abundance through him, and they all were blessed.

The remainder of Abraham's life is filled with stories of Abraham blessing the nations, providing water in dry places, living among garden trees, having many children, and even being buried in a place described like a garden. Abraham's trust opened the blessings of Eden to him. And through him, the nations around him received the blessing of Eden. But Abraham eventually died—someone who trusted God like Abraham, only better and without failure or death, would be needed to become God's image-bearing royal priest who would reenter Eden to set the cosmos right again.

*And He took him outside and said, "Now look
toward the heavens, and count the stars, if you
are able to count them." And He said to him, "So
shall your descendants be." Then he believed in
the LORD ; and He reckoned it to him as
righteousness.*

~ GENESIS 15:5–6

*But the angel of the LORD called to him from
heaven and said, "Abraham, Abraham!" And he
said, "Here I am." He said, "Do not stretch out
your hand against the lad, and do nothing to
him; for now I know that you fear God, since you
have not withheld your son, your only son, from
Me." Then Abraham raised his eyes and looked,
and behold, behind him a ram caught in the
thicket by his horns; and Abraham went and
took the ram and offered him up for a burnt
offering in the place of his son. Abraham called
the name of that place The LORD Will Provide, as
it is said to this day, "In the mount of the LORD it
will be provided."*

~ GENESIS 22:11–14

THE SHOOT OF JESSE

December 5
A MODEL RULER

As God promised, Abraham's son, Isaac, was the one to carry on Abraham's line. Isaac had two sons: Esau and Jacob. Jacob had four wives but only loved one of them. Between his wives, he had twelve sons, but he loved the firstborn of his favorite wife best. His name was Joseph.

Jacob spoiled Joseph, and Joseph became a bit of a brat. His brothers grew to hate him. One day, Joseph began to have dreams. In his dreams, he was mighty and glorified. His dreams placed him in such a high position that he even dreamt of his family bowing to him, and even the spiritual beings knelt before him. This was too much for his family to listen to. His parents rebuked him, but his brothers plotted against him. In the field, the brothers captured him and sold him as a slave to passing traders. They took his coat, dipped it in animal blood, and showed it to their parents to convince them that Joseph had been killed by wild beasts. They never expected to hear from Joseph again.

The traders took Joseph to Egypt, where they sold him to be the slave to a powerful man. God heard Joseph's cries for mercy. Joseph went from being a lowly slave to managing the entire household of one of the richest men in the land because God blessed everything Joseph did. But one day, someone accused Joseph of a crime he did not commit. Joseph had been righteous, but he ended up being thrown into prison.

In prison, Joseph found himself in another lowly position, just like when his brothers had sold him as a slave.

THE SHOOT OF JESSE

But Joseph chose to trust in God's plan and in His mercy. He remained righteous, and God continued to bless him. God blessed him so much that even the prison guards began to trust him with running parts of the prison. Soon, Joseph was in charge of managing much of the prison because God blessed Joseph because of the trust that he continued to place in God.

One night, two prisoners each had a dream. They told their dreams to Joseph, and God gave him the ability to know the meaning of their dreams so that he might bless them by revealing it. The dreams foretold that one would go free and the other would be put to death. These things happened just as Joseph had revealed. The one who was set free went to work in the palace of Pharaoh, king of Egypt, and he forgot about Joseph.

But, one day, Pharaoh had two dreams that deeply disturbed him. Nobody could help him to understand the meaning of his dreams. Suddenly, the man who had gone free from prison remembered Joseph! They brought Joseph from the prison to tell Pharaoh the meaning of the dreams. Again, God gave Joseph the ability to know the meaning of the dreams. Both dreams predicted that the land would have seven years of producing exceedingly more food than they could possibly need, followed by seven years when the entire world would hardly produce any food at all. Joseph revealed the meaning of the dreams to Pharaoh and suggested that Pharaoh should plan for the years of lack during the years of abundance.

Pharaoh didn't only like Joseph's plan, he liked Joseph himself. Joseph had found favor in Pharaoh's eyes,

R.A. SWEENEY

and he was placed as second-in-command of the entire kingdom. His main task was to collect food in preparation for the years of lack and manage the food stores during those bad years. Joseph did just that. He collected food for those years and stored it up so that during the years of lack they never ran out. During that time, the entire world sent people to Egypt to buy food. It was the refuge of abundance in a world without food. Even Joseph's brothers came to buy from him. Once they found out their brother was the one governing Egypt, they were reconciled. Pharaoh even gave an entire region of the land to Joseph's family so they could come live in the land of abundance. Joseph found so much favor with Pharaoh that when Joseph's father died, Pharaoh's princes led the funeral parade all the way back to Canaan.

Joseph was placed into hopeless situations several times in his life. But each time that he could have despaired, he instead chose to trust God and cry out to Him for rescue. Because of this trust, God continued to give Joseph more and more favor, until Joseph was ruling over the most powerful nation in the world and turned it into an Eden-like land of abundance and blessing for the world. But Joseph eventually died. He was not able to escape from death. The story leaves the world hoping for someone who would come in faith and trust, who could rule the nations in wisdom and obedience to God, like Joseph, but also be able to conquer death itself. Someone like Joseph, but better than Joseph, would be needed to rescue the world and restore the Eden kingdom.

THE SHOOT OF JESSE

I am your brother Joseph, whom you sold into Egypt. Now do not be grieved or angry with yourselves, because you sold me here, for God sent me before you to preserve life. For the famine has been in the land these two years, and there are still five years in which there will be neither plowing nor harvesting. God sent me before you to preserve for you a remnant in the earth, and to keep you alive by a great deliverance. Now, therefore, it was not you who sent me here, but God; and He has made me a father to Pharaoh and lord of all his household and ruler over all the land of Egypt.

~ GENESIS 45:4–8

R.A. SWEENEY

When Joseph's brothers saw that their father was dead, they said, "What if Joseph bears a grudge against us and pays us back in full for all the wrong which we did to him!" So they sent a message to Joseph, saying, "Your father charged before he died, saying, 'Thus you shall say to Joseph, "Please forgive, I beg you, the transgression of your brothers and their sin, for they did you wrong."' And now, please forgive the transgression of the servants of the God of your father." And Joseph wept when they spoke to him. Then his brothers also came and fell down before him and said, "Behold, we are your servants." But Joseph said to them, "Do not be afraid, for am I in God's place? As for you, you meant evil against me, but God meant it for good in order to bring about this present result, to preserve many people alive. So therefore, do not be afraid; I will provide for you and your little ones." So he comforted them and spoke kindly to them.

~ GENESIS 50:15–21

THE SHOOT OF JESSE

December 6
MOSES AND THE EXODUS

Joseph's whole family moved down to Egypt, seventy people in all (including Joseph's family who were already there). They lived there for about 400 years and grew into a huge people group (called Israelites), numbering in the millions. A new pharaoh was crowned king, and he did not know about Joseph or what his family had done for Egypt. He saw the Israelites as a threat. He enslaved the whole people of Israel with brutal forced labor, making bricks like the people in Babylon had done. The pharaoh also tried to have all of the Israelite sons killed by drowning them in the Nile River so they would not continue to grow in number. He was afraid the Israelites would turn against him and destroy his kingdom. What God had turned into a land of abundance and prosperity had now become a land of fear and death.

One of these Israelite baby boys escaped this pharaoh's plot to stop the growth of the Israelite people by being hidden in a wooden box floating in the waters of death. (This box is called the same Hebrew word that was used to describe Noah's ark.) God even sheltered him in Pharaoh's own house. His name was Moses. He later fled from Egypt to live in the wilderness of Midian. There, he married a wife and started a family. He worked for his wife's father tending sheep.

One day, while Moses was tending the sheep on a

THE SHOOT OF JESSE

mountain, God appeared to him as something that looked like fire in a small tree. God gave Moses a mission to go back to Egypt and demand that Pharaoh release the Israelites from slavery. God told Moses that Pharaoh would not agree to this. God would display His power in the land of Egypt and force Pharaoh to let the people go.

Reluctantly, Moses went back to Egypt. He went to Pharaoh and demanded the Israelites be set free. Pharaoh wouldn't listen. To display God's power, Moses gave himself a horrible skin disease and then healed it. He even turned a wooden staff into a terrible sea dragon before Pharaoh's own eyes. But Pharaoh was unconvinced and refused to let the Israelites go. Moses kept coming and demanding freedom for the people, but Pharaoh kept refusing. Each time, God used Moses as His instrument to unleash disasters upon Egypt. The Nile River turned to blood, as if the earth returned all the innocent blood Pharaoh had shed from the Israelite boys. Bugs and storms killed all the crops and livestock. The people were struck with sickness. The land was covered in darkness. Ten plagues were sent upon Egypt through Moses, meant to demonstrate God's ability to undo His work of creating the cosmos in Genesis 1 (a cosmos created by God speaking ten times).

Each time, Moses demanded the Israelites be freed or a new plague would come. Each time, Pharaoh would not allow it. Each time, the plague would come. Some of the times, Pharaoh would promise to let them go if Moses removed the plague. The other times, Moses removed the plague out of mercy. Each time, Pharaoh ultimately did not let them go. Ironically, it was not the Israelites that destroyed Egypt (as Pharaoh had feared), but Pharaoh's own hard heart. A final plague, the tenth, would be needed to change Pharaoh's heart. Just as Pharaoh had killed the baby boys of the Israelites, God would remove His protection from the land of Egypt and let Death itself come and take the lives of the firstborn son of every family in Egypt. No family was safe.

But God is not an unjust god. He gave a way of escape from the coming Death. Anyone who trusted in Him could take a lamb and kill it. They were to paint their door frame with the lamb's blood as a symbol that God had taken a life in place of their firstborn. They were also supposed to have a hurried feast of roasted lamb and flatbread. God promised to stand between Death and any house where the blood was on the door. This sign of protection was offered to anyone who would take it. Israelites who did not take God's way of escape were not protected, and non-Israelites who trusted God's way of escape and took it found the same protection God's faithful people received.

That night, Death passed through the land of Egypt and killed every firstborn male in the land. Only those in a house with lamb's blood around the door were spared. Pharaoh awoke to a cry of lament throughout the whole land. He sent messengers to Moses to drive the whole Israelite people from the land. But Pharaoh's heart was still hard. After he sent them out, he amassed his army to follow them into the wilderness and kill them there.

God led the Israelites and many non-Israelite people who decided to trust God to the Sea of Reeds. He had

THE SHOOT OF JESSE

Moses hold his wooden staff over the sea. God blew his breath across the sea and parted it so there was a pathway of dry land through the sea. The Israelites passed through the sea to the safety of the other side. The Egyptian army followed them into the sea. But God blew His breath once again. The sea crashed in on top of them, killing Pharaoh and his entire army.

To this day, Israelites celebrate the Festival of Passover to remember God rescuing them from Death, freeing them from harsh slavery, and destroying the Egyptian army that came to kill them. This is what deliverance from the Sin Serpent's kingdom by God's power looks like.

R.A. SWEENEY

The LORD *said, "I have surely seen the affliction of My people who are in Egypt, and have given heed to their cry because of their taskmasters, for I am aware of their sufferings. So I have come down to deliver them from the power of the Egyptians, and to bring them up from that land to a good and spacious land, to a land flowing with milk and honey, to the place of the Canaanite and the Hittite and the Amorite and the Perizzite and the Hivite and the Jebusite. Now, behold, the cry of the sons of Israel has come to Me; furthermore, I have seen the oppression with which the Egyptians are oppressing them. Therefore, come now, and I will send you to Pharaoh, so that you may bring My people, the sons of Israel, out of Egypt."*

~ EXODUS 3:7–10

THE SHOOT OF JESSE

For I will go through the land of Egypt on that night, and will strike down all the firstborn in the land of Egypt, both man and beast; and against all the gods of Egypt I will execute judgments—I am the LORD *. The blood shall be a sign for you on the houses where you live; and when I see the blood I will pass over you, and no plague will befall you to destroy you when I strike the land of Egypt.*

~ EXODUS 12:12–13

R.A. SWEENEY

But Moses said to the people, "Do not fear! Stand by and see the salvation of the LORD which He will accomplish for you today; for the Egyptians whom you have seen today, you will never see them again forever. The LORD will fight for you while you keep silent." Then the LORD said to Moses, "Why are you crying out to Me? Tell the sons of Israel to go forward. As for you, lift up your staff and stretch out your hand over the sea and divide it, and the sons of Israel shall go through the midst of the sea on dry land."

~ EXODUS 14:13–16

THE SHOOT OF JESSE

December 7
MOSES IN THE WILDERNESS

As the waters settled in the Sea of Reeds, Moses led the Israelites and everyone else who came with them in a song of worship to God. His brother and sister joined in to lead the entire people in the praising of God for His mighty works. But the celebration couldn't last long. Millions of people were in the middle of the wilderness without food, water, or shelter.

It did not take long for the people to begin to complain. God had done a mighty work, but they did not have what they needed in order to survive. So, the people considered returning to slavery and blamed God as cruel. Moses could not keep the people rejoicing in God for long.

The first complaint was a lack of water. The first waters they came to were described as *marim*, meaning they were not suitable for drinking. When the people complained, God gave Moses a method of miraculously cleansing the waters so they could be drunk. Then, the people complained about a lack of food. Moses prayed, and God began to rain down a seed-like substance from the heavens each morning. It was called *manna*, which means "What is it?" in Hebrew. The people could use the manna to make bread, and they ate their fill every day. The people soon got tired of eating only bread and complained about not having meat. Moses prayed, and God provided floods of quail every day for the people to eat. Then, there was

THE SHOOT OF JESSE

another issue of the people not trusting God to provide water, and Moses had to intercede again. The people kept complaining and trying to rebel. Moses managed to wrangle the people, but he could not keep them faithful.

The people continued their journey until they came to the foot of the mountain on which God originally appeared to Moses—Mount Sinai. God gave all the people an invitation to ascend the mountain and meet with God face-to-face. They were all invited to have personal relationships with God. The people were terrified and refused. They begged Moses to go up the mountain as their representative. Moses agreed. . . reluctantly.

Moses went up the mountain and met with God. God told Moses that if the people would commit themselves to Him in a faithful relationship, He would commit Himself to them as their faithful Provider and God. Moses took the message back down to the people and they all agreed. Moses took the response back up the mountain to God. He spent several days on the top of the mountain. God made good on His promise and started to provide for His people with a gift. God gave Moses the *Torah*, which means "instruction" in Hebrew. This was God's wisdom teaching on how to live a life that is filled with joy and abundance. But before Moses could bring this gift down to the people, they had already broken their agreement, made an idol statue of a calf made of gold, and began worshiping the statue.

Moses then had to go back up the mountain and intercede for the people. God was angry at the rejection by the people and wanted to abandon them as they had abandoned Him. A complete abandonment by God would leave the people dead. Moses begged God to spare the people and even offered his own life in place of the lives of the people. God did not accept Moses's offer of his life but agreed to forgive the people.

During this time, God also gave the people designs for the tabernacle. This was a big tent structure that God would use as His place to meet with His people. The designs made the entire space reminiscent of a garden, with imagery of trees and fruit and even incense and oils that smelled like sweet garden plants. It was like a little, portable Eden space. Moses would go in and meet with God face-to-face on behalf of the people since they refused to meet with Him on their own.

After spending a year at this mountain learning from God, the people then moved on to the Jordan River, across from the land God had promised to give them. They scouted out the land and found that God had a beautiful land of abundance planned for them, but that it was filled with giants and strong armies. They refused to trust God by entering the land He had promised them. Since they had rejected His land, God sent them to live out their lives in the wilderness until the next generation grew up.

While in the wilderness, the people continued to rebel against God. God had given them His wisdom teaching, but they refused to learn from it. The stories of rebellion at this point look similar to the ones on the way to Mount Sinai, only worse. They complained about water and food. They tried to remove Moses as their leader. Priests refused to follow God's rules for the priestly figures. Even

THE SHOOT OF JESSE

Moses's own siblings tried to take control from him.

Through it all, Moses continued to trust God. He led the people by personally living according to God's wisdom but could not get the people to obey God's wisdom teaching or to remain faithful to God. Ultimately, Moses died in the wilderness because of his own sins. He was not the one to take the throne in the garden.

R.A. SWEENEY

Yet He commanded the clouds above

And opened the doors of heaven;

He rained down manna upon them to eat

And gave them food from heaven.

Man did eat the bread of angels;

He sent them food in abundance.

He caused the east wind to blow in the heavens

And by His power He directed the south wind.

When He rained meat upon them like the dust,

Even winged fowl like the sand of the seas,

Then He let them fall in the midst of their camp,

Round about their dwellings.

So they ate and were well filled,

And their desire He gave to them.

Before they had satisfied their desire,

While their food was in their mouths,

The anger of God rose against them

And killed some of their stoutest ones,

And subdued the choice men of Israel.

In spite of all this they still sinned

And did not believe in His wonderful works.

~ PSALM 78:23–32

THE SHOOT OF JESSE

December 8
CONQUEST BY FAITH?

Before Moses died, the people of God were back at the Jordan River, preparing to enter into the land, and Moses appointed Joshua to be his replacement. Joshua was stepping up to the plate to be the leader of God's people.

When Moses died, God spoke to Joshua, telling him to be strong-spirited and firmly rooted. Joshua would lead the people in conquering the land that God promised, but the instruction God gave him was to trust God and remain in Him. He was not to be a mighty conqueror but an obedient observer of God's work.

The start of the conquest was a period of preparation for the people. God wanted the people to purify themselves before they entered the land. When it came time for them to entire the land, the Jordan River was raging. God told Joshua to have the priests carry the ark of God into the water. Just like at the Sea of Reeds, the waters were pushed back and piled in a heap so God's people could pass through on dry land.

On the other side of the river stood the fortress city of Jericho. God sent the commander of His army of spiritual beings to talk to Joshua before they attacked the city. The commander told Joshua they were only supposed to circle the city and praise God with shouts and blasts of ram's horn trumpets in the sight of the people of Jericho. As they did so, God's spiritual army attacked the city and destroyed the walls of the city. The people of God rushed in and destroyed the city without casualties.

THE SHOOT OF JESSE

Joshua then directed the army to the next town, Ai. But this time, when the army attacked, they were defeated terribly. Joshua regrouped the people, and they sought God about why they failed. Apparently, one person in the camp had stolen some valuables from Jericho that were supposed to be given to God. Moses, at Mount Sinai, had prayed for the rebels in the camp and offered his own life in their place. Joshua took a different strategy—he took the thief's whole family outside the camp, led the entire people of Israel in stoning them to death, and then burned all of their possessions. After this, the conquest went well. They moved throughout the entire land and took out most of the big cities and fortified places. Nobody could stand in their way, and the entire region was laid waste.

But Joshua ultimately proved to fail in his mission. While he attacked the major strong places in the land, he did not drive out all the people in the land like he had been commanded to. There were still smaller cities that had not been conquered and bands of refugees from the cities they had destroyed. The region was still unstable and filled with enemies of God's people.

Not only did Joshua stop short, but he also was tricked by the people of the land. A region of the land, called Gibeah, sent messengers to Joshua to make a peace treaty. They made themselves look like they were from far away and had traveled a great distance. They told Joshua they were from a distant land that had heard about God's power and wanted a peace treaty. Joshua didn't ask who they were or what this distant land was. He simply agreed to the terms. Later, he found out that the people of Gibeah were one of the tribes that he was supposed to destroy, but he could not because he had promised to be at peace with them.

The people had entered the land, but it was a rocky start. They had conquered the strongholds, but there remained leaderless bands of soldiers hiding all over the land. Joshua did not lead in wisdom, and the people groups he was supposed to subdue had subdued him through deceit. God's people were still rebellious and only remained faithful because punishment for disobedience was strict.

Joshua was a fairly successful military leader, but he was far from perfect. Under his leadership, the people were obedient to the rules, but they did not develop personal relationships of love and intimacy with God. He was not God's image-bearing royal priest either. The search continued.

THE SHOOT OF JESSE

Be strong and courageous, for you shall give this people possession of the land which I swore to their fathers to give them. Only be strong and very courageous; be careful to do according to all the law which Moses My servant commanded you; do not turn from it to the right or to the left, so that you may have success wherever you go. This book of the law shall not depart from your mouth, but you shall meditate on it day and night, so that you may be careful to do according to all that is written in it; for then you will make your way prosperous, and then you will have success. Have I not commanded you? Be strong and courageous! Do not tremble or be dismayed, for the LORD your God is with you wherever you go.

~ JOSHUA 1:6–9

R.A. SWEENEY

Now Joshua was old and advanced in years when the LORD said to him, "You are old and advanced in years, and very much of the land remains to be possessed."

~ JOSHUA 13:1

THE SHOOT OF JESSE

December 9
CYCLES OF SIN

During Moses's life, Joshua was his assistant. Moses spent years trying to shape Joshua into the next leader of Israel. Joshua ended up being a very different leader than Moses, and Joshua never trained up someone to replace him. After Joshua, there was not a distinct leader for Israel. Without a leader, the people were left to guide themselves in their relationship with God. Everyone did what looked good in their own eyes.[6]

The people fell into a repeating cycle during this time. As God blessed the people with abundance, the people began to turn away from God. In their abundance, they did not see a need for God. They, then, would worship idols and turn away from God's ways. As the people descended into wickedness, God allowed them to walk away from Him. Without His protection and blessing, the enemies of the Israelites would overwhelm them and oppress them. As their oppression became unbearable, the people would remember the God who rescued them out of oppression in Egypt and would cry out to God. God is the type of god who cannot stand to watch oppression. So, when His people cried out in their oppression, He would raise up someone, called a *judge*, to be a rescuer for the people. This person would deliver the Israelites from oppression and would typically rule over the people until he died. During that time, the people would follow God as best as they could, but once the leader was gone, they would turn back away from God. The cycle would start over again and again.

THE SHOOT OF JESSE

At first, the judges simply united the tribes to drive the oppressors from their land. Then, they started to become violent warriors. After the first couple of judges, a judge arose who was a secret assassin. He used deception to slither into the room of the king who was oppressing God's people and kill him. When the next judge arose, the only thing we are told is that he killed hundreds of people. God uses the people available to Him, and as the people became more and more wicked, His chosen tools became less and less righteous.

The next judge, Barak, was a little better. There was a prophetess named Deborah during that time who spoke God's word to Israel and helped them to seek Him. Deborah summoned Barak to her and told him that God had appointed him to lead the armies of Israel to defeat their oppressors. Barak was scared. He knew he was not the right person to lead Israel and that he needed God with him if he was going to be successful. He could have listened to Deborah say that God had appointed him and trusted God in that, but Barak demanded that Deborah go with him. He saw Deborah as God's presence. With Deborah, Barak led the people to victory, but he was still a very flawed spiritual leader for the people.

The next judges kept getting worse. Gideon was another coward, whom God eventually convinced to lead the people. They defeated their enemies, but then Gideon's rage caused him to kill some of their own people for not helping him. Once he had secured peace, he tried to make his family a dynasty of kings. His sons fought each other and murdered each other. Gideon was not great, but his kids led the people into wickedness again.

Then came Jephthah. He was an outlaw, who led a band of criminals that lived in the wilderness robbing and plundering. When the people were oppressed, they went to him to lead them. The outlaw leader who robbed them was their best choice of leader. He did lead them to victory, but then he offered his own daughter as a sacrifice to God (something God has never wanted) and led a war against one of the Israelite tribes.

Samson was the last judge in the story. God gave him superhuman strength, but he became a murderous rage-monster. He deceived people to steal from them and killed any time he felt wronged. He was even flippant with his God-given power and eventually lost it. In the end, he was successful in striking a mighty blow against God's enemies, taking their temple down upon the heads of their leaders and nobles, but he was killed in the process and did nothing to unite the Israelites or lead them to be faithful to God.

The end of the book of Judges gives a couple of pictures of what the people were like during this time. The theme of the book is that they had no king during that time, and the judges failed to lead the people. Without a righteous king, the people stole and killed, worshiped idols, and became immoral in every way. They needed a king.

THE SHOOT OF JESSE

*Then the sons of Israel did evil in the sight of the
LORD and served the Baals, and they forsook the
LORD , the God of their fathers, who had brought
them out of the land of Egypt, and followed other
gods from among the gods of the peoples who
were around them, and bowed themselves down
to them; thus they provoked the LORD to anger.
So they forsook the LORD and served Baal and
the Ashtaroth. The anger of the LORD burned
against Israel, and He gave them into the hands
of plunderers who plundered them; and He sold
them into the hands of their enemies around
them, so that they could no longer stand before
their enemies. Wherever they went, the hand of
the LORD was against them for evil, as the LORD
had spoken and as the LORD had sworn to them,
so that they were severely distressed. Then the
LORD raised up judges who delivered them from
the hands of those who plundered them. Yet they
did not listen to their judges, for they played the
harlot after other gods and bowed themselves
down to them. They turned aside quickly from
the way in which their fathers had walked in
obeying the commandments of the LORD; ...*

R.A. SWEENEY

they did not do as their fathers. When the LORD *raised up judges for them, the* LORD *was with the judge and delivered them from the hand of their enemies all the days of the judge; for the* LORD *was moved to pity by their groaning because of those who oppressed and afflicted them. But it came about when the judge died, that they would turn back and act more corruptly than their fathers, in following other gods to serve them and bow down to them; they did not abandon their practices or their stubborn ways.*

~ JUDGES 2:11–19

In those days there was no king in Israel; everyone did what was right in his own eyes.

~ JUDGES 21:25

THE SHOOT OF JESSE

December 10
LOYAL LOVE

During the time of the judges, a man, his wife, and their two sons lived in Bethlehem in Israel. There was a famine in the land, so they left the land God had promised to bless them in and moved to the land of Moab, a people who were enemies of God's people. They abandoned their people and their God in order to seek blessing elsewhere.

Once they settled in Moab, the husband, whose name was *Elimelekh* ("God is King"), died. His two sons, *Makh'lon* ("Sicko") and *Khil'yon* ("Wasting-Away"), married Moabite women, but the sons died as well. The three women were left without husbands or sons. In this culture, they were in trouble. Men were the ones who earned money and provided for the family. A woman who was separated from any working-aged men would be helpless. Three of them together would be hopeless. Their lives were over.

Naomi, the mother, gathered her two daughters-in-law, Orpah and Ruth, and told them to return to their fathers' houses to be rescued from the certain death that followed her. She could not offer them life or prosperity, so she wanted to release them from her so that they might live. They all cried over the situation, and Orpah kissed Naomi goodbye, but Ruth clung to Naomi in love. She promised Naomi that she would follow her wherever she went in life or in death. She would remain loyal to her mother-in-law no matter the cost. She would not leave Naomi to die alone. Naomi saw that Ruth could not be dissuaded and led Ruth back to Judah.

THE SHOOT OF JESSE

When they returned, they still owned their former land. They had a place to live, but no way to earn money or grow food. Their only opportunity was through begging. In Israel, the poor were legally allowed to harvest the edges of anyone's fields or keep anything the harvesters dropped in the fields. This was called *gleaning*, and it was a practice God gifted to His people so that even the poorest people had a chance to work for their own food. Ruth took this as her method of providing for her mother-in-law.

God directed Ruth to a specific field, owned by a man named Boaz, who was very wealthy. She gleaned in that field and was treated well by the workers of the field. Boaz came out into the field to check on his workers and asked about the young woman in the field. Boaz had heard the news of Naomi returning without her family but with a young woman who showed her extreme loyal love. When Boaz discovered this was the young woman who loved his kinswoman so dearly, he wanted to bless her. He begged her to only glean from his field. She would be kept safe, and he would get to see her every day. He directed his harvesters to "accidentally" leave grain in the field so she could collect it, and he gave her gifts of grain as well. She was welcomed and treated generously because she was so generously faithful to Naomi.

When Naomi heard where Ruth had been gleaning and of the favor that Boaz had shown her, she directed Ruth to ask Boaz for a specific favor. In Israel, there was another practice to provide for the poor. If the men of a family died without sons, a relative, called a kinsman redeemer, was required to buy the deceased's property, marry the widow, and raise a family in the name of the dead man so that his name would not die out. Boaz was a close relative, so Naomi instructed Ruth to ask Boaz to redeem them.

When Ruth asked, Boaz was overjoyed at the idea. Ruth had demonstrated her faithfulness and loyal love for Naomi so wonderfully that she was not only beautiful in Boaz's eyes, but irresistible. He didn't just have a requirement to redeem them; he wanted to. The only problem was that there was a closer relative, and he was the one with the first right and responsibility to redeem. Boaz was so enchanted by Ruth's faithfulness that he was determined to make sure that she was redeemed.

Early the next day, Boaz went and waited for the other relative, whom the Bible names something along the lines of Mr. So-and-so. Boaz presented Mr. So-and-so with the opportunity to buy the property that now belonged to Naomi. This was a huge cost, but Mr. So-and-so was willing to expend the money. Next, Boaz presented the other part of the redemption, marrying Ruth and raising a son in the name of Naomi's late husband. This cost was too great in Mr. So-and-so's eyes, and he decided he would not live up to the expectation and would not provide for the widows. He refused his right and obligation, and he offered it to Boaz instead. Inspired by Ruth's loyal love for Naomi, there was no cost too great for him to redeem the woman he loved.

Boaz spared no expense to redeem his beloved because her loyal love for Naomi inspired his loyal love for her. They had a son, and his name was Obed.

THE SHOOT OF JESSE

*But Ruth said, "Do not urge me to leave you or turn back from following you; for where you go, I will go, and where you lodge, I will lodge. Your people shall be my people, and your God, my God. Where you die, I will die, and there I will be buried. Thus may the L*ORD *do to me, and worse, if anything but death parts you and me."*

~ RUTH 1:16–17

*Boaz replied to her, "All that you have done for your mother-in-law after the death of your husband has been fully reported to me, and how you left your father and your mother and the land of your birth, and came to a people that you did not previously know. May the L*ORD *reward your work, and your wages be full from the L*ORD*, the God of Israel, under whose wings you have come to seek refuge."*

~ RUTH 2:11–12

R.A. SWEENEY

Then the women said to Naomi, "Blessed is the
Lord who has not left you without a redeemer
today, and may his name become famous in
Israel. May he also be to you a restorer of life and
a sustainer of your old age; for your daughter-in-
law, who loves you and is better to you than
seven sons, has given birth to him."

~ Ruth 4:14–15

THE SHOOT OF JESSE

December 11
HEARING FROM GOD

Shortly after the time of Ruth and Boaz, another Israelite woman, named Hannah, was in distress. She was one of her husband's two wives. The other wife had many children, but Hannah could not have children. The other wife teased her terribly, and Hannah grieved in her shame. One day, Hannah went to the Tabernacle of God to offer sacrifices, and she sat down to pray. In her desperation, Hannah closed her eyes and mouthed the words of her prayer.

At that same time, the high priest, Eli, was at the door of the tabernacle. Eli was not a righteous man. He was neglectful in his duties, and his sons were wicked and abused their positions as priests. Eli knew the sins of his sons and allowed them to continue anyway. As Eli stood there, watching a woman sitting at the tabernacle courtyard mouthing words to herself, he could not even recognize what distressed prayer looked like. Eli thought she was drunk and rebuked her. His life was so far separated from a relationship with God that he could not recognize what a relationship with God actually looked like. Nevertheless, Hannah told Eli she wanted a son, and Eli told her she would return the next year with a son.

Hannah did go on to get pregnant and have a son, and she named him *Samuel* (which means "God hears"). As Samuel grew into a child, Hannah brought him back to the tabernacle. She had promised God that if He gave her a son, she would give him to the Lord as His servant. Hannah brought Samuel back to the tabernacle and left him to be raised as a priest, but she continued to visit and sent gifts to

THE SHOOT OF JESSE

her treasured child.

Samuel grew into a young man and served as a priest in the tabernacle. At that time, God rarely spoke to the people or gave visions because His priest was not faithful. But one night, as Samuel lay sleeping, he heard a voice calling him. He ran to Eli to ask what Eli wanted, but Eli did not know what Samuel was talking about and sent Samuel back to bed. Again, Samuel awoke to a voice calling to him. Again, he ran to Eli. Again, Eli did not know what Samuel was talking about and sent him back to bed. When it happened a third time, Eli finally figured out what was happening. He sent Samuel back to bed again, but this time with instruction to respond to the voice if it came again. Samuel heard the voice a fourth time and responded to the voice, "Speak, for Your servant is listening."[7]

God spoke to Samuel about the downfall of Eli and his family because of their wickedness. In the morning, Eli asked Samuel what God had spoken to him and Samuel told Eli. He told Eli about God's condemnation of the sins of Eli's family and told him that his whole family would die all at once. At this moment, Samuel became God's prophet. Everything happened as God had said through Samuel.

As God's priest and prophet, Samuel became the last judge of Israel. When the Philistines, the enemies of the Israelites, brought an army to invade Israel, the people of Israel went to Samuel to deliver them just as they had done with the previous judges. Samuel gathered the people together at a place called Mitz'pah ("Watchtower"), where years before Abraham's grandson had made peace with a deceitful neighbor. There, Samuel led the people in a communal confession of sins and prayer for rescue. In response to the people truly humbling themselves in repentance and begging for deliverance, God sent a thunderstorm against the Philistine army. This storm was so great it defeated the army, and they ran scared back to their homes. Apparently, the storm was so terrifying that those Philistines who fled from it were too scared to ever invade Israel again for the rest of their lives.

Samuel had brought the people together to humble themselves before God and to seek His favor. After the battle, Samuel directed the people to set up a giant monolith stone as a reminder to them that their God is a deliverer for those who seek Him and repent of their sins. This was a visual reminder for them and their children of the blessings of following God. Samuel then continually traveled a circular route throughout the land so that people could seek God's wisdom through him in all parts of Israel.

This was what a judge was supposed to be. Instead of being a great military leader, Samuel led the people in being still and trusting in God's deliverance, just as Moses had done at the Sea of Reeds or Joshua had done at Jericho. Samuel sought after God and led the people in doing the same. He was a true spiritual leader for the people. Unfortunately, Samuel's sons did not take after him, and they instead acted like Eli's wicked sons. When Samuel grew old, there was no righteous leader to take over.

THE SHOOT OF JESSE

Thus Samuel grew and the LORD *was with him and let none of his words fail. All Israel from Dan even to Beersheba knew that Samuel was confirmed as a prophet of the* LORD. *And the* LORD *appeared again at Shiloh, because the* LORD *revealed Himself to Samuel at Shiloh by the word of the* LORD.

~ 1 SAMUEL 3:19–21

R.A. SWEENEY

Now Samuel judged Israel all the days of his life. He used to go annually on circuit to Bethel and Gilgal and Mizpah, and he judged Israel in all these places. Then his return was to Ramah, for his house was there, and there he judged Israel; and he built there an altar to the LORD.

~ 1 SAMUEL 7:15–17

THE SHOOT OF JESSE

December 12
THE CORRUPTION OF KINGS

Samuel was getting older, and public confidence in his sons was minimal. The people of Israel went to Samuel to ask for a king. They told him that they were scared of what would happen when Samuel died. They were worried they would not continue to follow God without Samuel, and that their enemies would come destroy them. They wanted a king so they could be like all the other nations. This was heartbreaking news for Samuel, and he went to God in prayer. God told Samuel that they were not rejecting Samuel as their prophet but rejecting God Himself as their God. God told him to give them a warning about all the terrible things that would happen if they picked a king, but that, if the people insisted on having a king, Samuel should give them a king.

Meanwhile, a man, named Kish, from the tribe of Benjamin, had a donkey wander off, so he sent his son, Saul, to go find it. While out looking for the donkey, Saul's path crossed with Samuel's. God had warned Samuel that he would come across the one he should anoint as king in this way. Samuel anointed Saul and told him he would become the king of Israel. All that was needed was to bring the people together to make Saul's kingship official.

Samuel summoned all the people together for the ceremony. He wanted to show all Israel that God had chosen Saul. Once all the people were assembled and sorted

THE SHOOT OF JESSE

among their tribes and houses, Samuel cast lots to pick the tribe. Saul's tribe was chosen. Then, Samuel cast lots to pick the family, and Saul's was chosen. The lots continued to whittle down the people until Saul was chosen as the king. Samuel called out to the crowd to summon Saul to the front, but he was nowhere to be found. The people had to search for him, and they found him hiding amid the people's piled baggage. This was the chosen king, the one who would lead the people against their enemies, hiding like a scared child.

Saul kept Samuel close by at all times. While Samuel advised Saul, the people prospered. The Ammonites attacked the Israelites and Saul led the army to a glorious victory. When the Philistines attacked, Saul and his son, Jonathan, won victories and fame. While Samuel was by his side, Saul enacted laws to govern the people in righteousness and enforced Torah compliance. As long as Samuel was with Saul, things went very well.

But as the Philistines assembled for war at Michmash, Samuel gave instruction for Saul to wait for him before fighting. He said he would be there on the seventh day. But on the morning of the seventh day, the soldiers began to flee in fear, and Saul lost his patience. He offered sacrifices to God (which was required to be done by a priest) out of desperation and fear and prepared to fight the battle. But just then, Samuel arrived and saw that Saul was not waiting. He proclaimed that, because Saul was not faithful to God, Saul's kingdom would not last. God was going to find a new king to take over once Saul died. Samuel went to find the new king and left Saul to rule on his own, since he was not interested in obeying God.

R.A. SWEENEY

Saul's disobedience and rejection of God brought disaster on the people. We are told that for the rest of Saul's reign there never ceased to be war between Israel and at least one of their neighbors. During one battle, Saul made a vow to kill anyone who ate anything until the battle was over and nearly had to kill his son. At every turn, he is depicted as the worst parts of the judges.

The last time that Samuel helped Saul was when the Amalekites were attacking. Samuel told Saul to take the army and attack them, but to destroy everything and everyone. Saul went and won the victory, but he did not kill their king (whose descendant almost killed the entire people of Israel), and they kept all the animals for food and property. Samuel again condemned Saul's disobedience. This time, God took away Saul's position as king. Saul remained king in the eyes of the people but not in God's eyes.

The rest of Saul's life was a whirlwind of disaster. He was constantly fighting wars and hunting down people he imagined to be traitors. He ruined relationships with his soldiers and his family. After Samuel's death, when things became really bad in the land, Saul went to a witch to summon Samuel's spirit from the dead in the hopes that Samuel's spirit would pray to God for him or speak God's word to him. Saul continued to sin more and more, and greater and greater disaster fell upon the land and his people.

The Philistines again brought an army against Israel. Saul led his army against them. Saul and his sons fought against the Philistines, and all of them died there. The first king of Israel was a complete failure.

THE SHOOT OF JESSE

R.A. SWEENEY

Has the LORD *as much delight in burnt offerings*
and sacrifices
As in obeying the voice of the LORD?
Behold, to obey is better than sacrifice,
And to heed than the fat of rams.
For rebellion is as the sin of divination,
And insubordination is as iniquity and idolatry.
Because you have rejected the word of the LORD *,*
He has also rejected you from being king.

~ 1 SAMUEL 15:22–23

THE SHOOT OF JESSE

December 13
THE MAN AFTER GOD'S OWN HEART

Before fighting the Philistines at Michmash, Saul failed to wait on God's timing. Because he was afraid, Saul decided to perform the priestly duties before the battle instead of waiting for Samuel to come. Because of this, Samuel told Saul that the kingdom would not pass on to Saul's son. Instead, God would find another man who desired the same things as God and would make him king.

God sent Samuel to the town of Bethlehem to find a man named Jesse. Jesse was the son of Obed, who was the son of Ruth and Boaz. God told Samuel that one of Jesse's sons was the man He had selected. Jesse gathered his sons and presented them, one by one, before Samuel. The firstborn was the obvious choice, and he looked like a king too. But as Jesse brought out one son after the next, God told Samuel they were not who He had chosen. When Samuel asked if Jesse had any more sons, Jesse brought in the young runt of the family, named David. Samuel immediately knew that this was the one God had chosen, and he anointed David as the next king of Israel right there.

But, while Saul was still king, David remained patient. He even became a servant of Saul. In all things, David loved God and tried to follow and obey Him. Because David pursued God with his entire heart, God blessed everything David did.

While David was still a young man, the Philistines

THE SHOOT OF JESSE

came against Israel at the Valley of Elah. They had a huge warrior, named Goliath, who hurled insults across the valley, demeaning God and His people. Goliath was described as a man of giant stature, like the violent giants before the flood. His armor was made of bronze scales. (The Hebrew word *nekhoshet*, rendered as "bronze" looks like their word *nakhash*, rendered as "serpent.") He was even described in Hebrew as a "man of the in-between," like the serpent that crossed boundaries in the Garden of Eden. This man was the Serpent's warrior. He offered a challenge to fight against Israel's champion and settle the battle between the two champions, rather than the entire armies fighting. No Israelite was willing to fight Goliath because he was so big and scary. David heard the insults and took up Goliath's challenge. God empowered him to kill the giant using a sling, stones, and the giant's own sword. David became a mighty warrior for God and a leader of many other mighty warriors.

As Saul continued to rebel against God, God allowed a madness to fall upon Saul. God had empowered David with a soothing and quieting ability for music. Saul brought David into his service to play music for Saul during his fits of madness. David's God-empowered musical abilities were able to soothe Saul out of his madness. David, in his passion for God, wrote dozens of songs to God, and much of the book of Psalms was written by him. David became a skillful worshiper of God and led many people in the worship of God.

But David's life was not all blessings. Saul became jealous of David and tried to kill him. When David fled from Saul, Saul hunted David and his followers for years. David had to go into hiding and live in the wilderness for years, even though God had promised he was the new king. David even had the chance to kill Saul twice, but both times he sought to be reconciled with his enemy rather than killing him. David was a man who sought peace and reconciliation, and he patiently trusted in God's timing.

After Saul's death, David became king. He was a generous and passionate king and was adored by his people. David led the army to capture the city of Jerusalem and set it up as the capital city of Israel. He brought the ark of God into Jerusalem so that God might be in the City of the King. David's joy in God was so great that he danced in front of the ark the entire way it was being brought into the city. He gave gifts and celebration to the entire nation.

What is amazing is that David made sacrifices to God along the way as the ark was being moved. When Saul made sacrifices to God, the kingdom was taken from him because he was afraid and did something that was not lawful. But David took the priestly role upon himself out of a love and passion for God and was blessed for it.

In that time, David made God's kingdom a reality on earth. He made a beautiful city with God's presence at the center. He expanded the boundaries of the kingdom to their second largest. He made peace with all of their neighboring nations. And, most importantly, David ruled over the people with justice, mercy, and generosity, even going to great lengths and expense to reconcile with people he had personally hurt or wronged.

But King David was far from perfect. He did many

THE SHOOT OF JESSE

bad things as well. He disobeyed God's command, refused to dispense justice against his own family when they were caught in sin, and even had his friend killed in order to marry the friend's wife. All of this brought death, brokenness, and even civil war to the nation. But when David failed, he repented. He spared no expense to right his wrongs with people or with God. His repentance stood out as a symbol of his godliness just as much as his faithfulness did. But his sins did lead to his death. A new king like him was needed, only better.

When they entered, he looked at Eliab and thought, "Surely the LORD's anointed is before Him." But the LORD said to Samuel, "Do not look at his appearance or at the height of his stature, because I have rejected him; for God sees not as man sees, for man looks at the outward appearance, but the LORD looks at the heart." Then Jesse called Abinadab and made him pass before Samuel. And he said, "The LORD has not chosen this one either." . . .

R.A. SWEENEY

*Next Jesse made Shammah pass by. And he said,
"The LORD has not chosen this one either." Thus
Jesse made seven of his sons pass before Samuel.
But Samuel said to Jesse, "The LORD has not
chosen these." And Samuel said to Jesse, "Are
these all the children?" And he said, "There
remains yet the youngest, and behold, he is
tending the sheep." Then Samuel said to Jesse,
"Send and bring him; for we will not sit down
until he comes here." So he sent and brought him
in. Now he was ruddy, with beautiful eyes and a
handsome appearance. And the LORD said,
"Arise, anoint him; for this is he." Then Samuel
took the horn of oil and anointed him in the
midst of his brothers; and the Spirit of the LORD
came mightily upon David from that day
forward.*

~ 1 SAMUEL 16:6–13

THE SHOOT OF JESSE

Then David took hold of his clothes and tore them, and so also did all the men who were with him. They mourned and wept and fasted until evening for Saul and his son Jonathan and for the people of the LORD and the house of Israel, because they had fallen by the sword.

~ 2 SAMUEL 1:11–12

R.A. SWEENEY

David went and brought up the ark of God from the house of Obed-edom into the city of David with gladness. And so it was, that when the bearers of the ark of the LORD had gone six paces, he sacrificed an ox and a fatling. And David was dancing before the LORD with all his might.

~ 2 SAMUEL 6:12–14

THE SHOOT OF JESSE

December 14
THE MAN OF PEACE

David had many sons, but before he died, he appointed his son, *Solomon* (which means "Man of Peace"), to be the next king. Solomon's story runs all over the place.

Before David died, he left instructions for Solomon to kill a bunch of people who had wronged David. This was the first act we see Solomon perform as king after David died. So much for being the man of peace. He also made an alliance with Egypt by marrying the pharaoh's daughter, something expressly forbidden by God's Torah, which Solomon was supposed to know and obey. Solomon was not off to a great start as God's chosen king.

Next, however, we are told Solomon went to a false altar but offered one thousand burnt offerings to God. This was a huge demonstration of devotion to God. But even in that demonstration, Solomon did not do things God's way. After offering the sacrifices, God appeared to Solomon in a dream. He told Solomon to ask for anything he wanted. Whether this was a blank check to receive anything he asked for is up for debate, but God at least wanted to hear the request. Solomon asked for the wisdom to rule God's people in a way that would honor and glorify God. God was pleased with this request and granted Solomon greater wisdom than any man who had yet walked the earth. He also promised to bless Solomon with long life and riches as well since Solomon's request was so praiseworthy.

Solomon did become the wisest man who had ever lived. He was able to rule the people with discernment and

THE SHOOT OF JESSE

issued wise judgments in legal cases he judged. His wisdom amazed his own people, and word traveled across the world. His wisdom became so well-known that a pagan queen from the southern parts of the world brought a caravan to Jerusalem just so she could meet the king and give him gifts. She stayed in Jerusalem until her curiosity about him could be satisfied. During that time, she asked him questions and riddles, and she presented him with all manner of challenges, but Solomon had wise answers to everything. When she was finally satisfied, she left, praising God for His amazing wisdom. The world marveled at God's wisdom because of Solomon.

Solomon also became the richest man in the world at that time. He expanded the borders of Israel to the largest they have ever been. He had peace with all of his neighboring countries. In this, he finally did become the man of peace. The people grew in number like never before. He imported all manner of precious metals, fine gems, and expensive oddities from all over the world. It is said that during his reign, silver was as common as stone[8], and every man had his own little personal Eden-like garden[9], from one end of the nation to the other. The world saw the riches of the kingdom of Israel and marveled at the God who could provide such wealth.

Solomon also did much to glorify God. He was extravagant in his offerings. He wrote many of the proverbs we now have in the book of Proverbs. But most importantly, Solomon commissioned the building of the temple in Jerusalem. He paid to have the temple built, furnished it with everything it would need, had the ark of

God moved into the temple, and celebrated a huge dedication feast with hundreds of thousands of sacrifices made. Solomon's capital became the center of the worship of God in the entire world.

But all through the story, there were hints of unfaithfulness to God, though God remained faithful to him. Solomon did not just marry the pharaoh's daughter; he took many wives from all over the world. All total, between his official wives and his unofficial wives, Solomon had 1,000 wives, most of whom were pagan women used to secure alliances with pagan nations. Solomon also amassed a huge standing army with powerful chariots and the best horses in the world. This was also something forbidden by God's Torah. We also are told that the temple's builders and the people sourcing materials were largely slave labor. He collected huge personal wealth and built for himself a mighty throne to assert his dominance over anyone who came before him. Solomon was guilty of breaking every command God had given the people about things the king should not do.

Over time, as Solomon became richer, as Israel became more powerful, as Solomon made more and more alliances with pagans, and as Solomon continued to marry pagan women, Solomon began to turn his back on God. By the time of his death, Solomon had completely rejected God and only worshiped pagan gods. The man of peace had failed like all the rest.

THE SHOOT OF JESSE

God said to him, "Because you have asked this thing and have not asked for yourself long life, nor have asked riches for yourself, nor have you asked for the life of your enemies, but have asked for yourself discernment to understand justice, behold, I have done according to your words. Behold, I have given you a wise and discerning heart, so that there has been no one like you before you, nor shall one like you arise after you. I have also given you what you have not asked, both riches and honor, so that there will not be any among the kings like you all your days. If you walk in My ways, keeping My statutes and commandments, as your father David walked, then I will prolong your days."

~ 1 KINGS 3:11–14

When you enter the land which the LORD your God gives you, and you possess it and live in it, and you say, "I will set a king over me like all the nations who are around me," you shall surely set a king over you whom the LORD your God . . .

R.A. SWEENEY

chooses, one from among your countrymen you shall set as king over yourselves; you may not put a foreigner over yourselves who is not your countryman. Moreover, he shall not multiply horses for himself, nor shall he cause the people to return to Egypt to multiply horses, since the LORD has said to you, "You shall never again return that way." He shall not multiply wives for himself, or else his heart will turn away; nor shall he greatly increase silver and gold for himself. Now it shall come about when he sits on the throne of his kingdom, he shall write for himself a copy of this law on a scroll in the presence of the Levitical priests. It shall be with him and he shall read it all the days of his life, that he may learn to fear the LORD his God, by carefully observing all the words of this law and these statutes, that his heart may not be lifted up above his countrymen and that he may not turn aside from the commandment, to the right or the left, so that he and his sons may continue long in his kingdom in the midst of Israel.

~ DEUTERONOMY 17:14–20

THE SHOOT OF JESSE

December 15
KINGDOM DIVIDED

Solomon is remembered as a great king. In fact, Solomon did many wonderful and praiseworthy things, and the kingdom prospered under his reign more than at any other time. But the sins that were used to build this empire were the seeds of the kingdom's own destruction.

Once Solomon died and his son took the throne, the people came to the new king and asked him to show them mercy. They were worn out from the forced labor and heavy taxes Solomon had used to build his great army, palaces, and other extravagances. They asked for the new king to lighten the load. The new king refused, and the people rebelled. Ten of the twelve tribes of Israel took a new king, named Jeroboam, and declared themselves a new nation, which they called Israel. The kingdom ruled by Solomon's son was named Judah.

Jeroboam was an intelligent man. He knew that if his people continued to regularly return to Jerusalem to visit God's temple, they would eventually go back to being ruled by Solomon's son, and Jeroboam would soon be a king without a people. To combat this threat to his power, Jeroboam set up two temples in Israel. In each temple, Jeroboam set up huge golden statues of calves for the people to worship. In this way, Jeroboam led the people away from God's kingdom and from the worship of God.

As soon as Jeroboam began setting up his temples, God sent prophets to warn him about this wickedness he was committing. One prophet told him not to rebel against

THE SHOOT OF JESSE

"

God in this way. Jeroboam stretched out his hand toward the prophet in anger but found his hand was decaying. He begged God for mercy through the prophet, and he was restored, but even this did not stop him from establishing idolatry in his kingdom.

Jeroboam was exceedingly wicked during his reign. And after him, his son, Nadab, took the throne. Nadab continued to lead the people in wickedness until a man named Ba'asha killed Nadab and Jeroboam's entire family. Then, Ba'asha took the throne. He was no better and even made war against David's family in Judah. Ba'asha's son also became king and was killed, along with Ba'asha's entire family, by another military leader. The people of Israel killed the man who killed Ba'asha's son as an assassin and took another king, but violence was leading to more violence, and wickedness was leading to more wickedness.

In the land of Judah, things did not go much better. Solomon's son led the people in idolatry as well. He set up shrines to all the pagan gods all throughout his land. His wickedness led to the nation of Egypt bringing an army against him. They came against Jerusalem and carried off all the wealth of the city. All of Solomon's prosperity was taken out in a single generation. And Solomon's grandson took the throne of Judah after Solomon's son died. He was no better than his father, and he continued to lead the people in worshiping pagan gods.

It was not until Solomon's great-grandson, Asa, took the throne that there was some semblance of repentance. Asa was said to have loved God with his whole heart, just like David had done, but he was not as successful at leading the people in following God. He stopped much of the practice of pagan idol worship, but he did not take down the pagan shrines. At that time, during Ba'asha's reign in Israel, he was constantly at war with Israel. To help fight the war, Asa made agreements with his pagan neighbors to fight with him against Israel. This was against God's commands that He had given to Moses and also came back to cause trouble for Judah later on. Asa was a good king who loved God, but he failed to keep God's commandments or lead his people in worshiping God.

Saul was the first king of God's people, and he was a huge failure. David was the second king, and he had great success in building God's kingdom, though his own sins caused him to ultimately fail in his mission. Solomon was the third king. He managed to grow the kingdom in size, power, and prosperity, but had also corrupted the entire kingdom into wickedness and idolatry. After that, the kingdom crumbled. Three generations of kings were all it took for the kingship to fall apart and fail. After Solomon, the kingdom divided, and idolatry ran rampant. Violence became a constant plague on God's people, and there was no longer any semblance of stability in the kingdoms.

THE SHOOT OF JESSE

Jeroboam said in his heart, "Now the kingdom will return to the house of David. If this people go up to offer sacrifices in the house of the LORD at Jerusalem, then the heart of this people will return to their lord, even to Rehoboam king of Judah; and they will kill me and return to Rehoboam king of Judah." So the king consulted, and made two golden calves, and he said to them, "It is too much for you to go up to Jerusalem; behold your gods, O Israel, that brought you up from the land of Egypt." He set one in Bethel, and the other he put in Dan.

~ 1 KINGS 12:26–29

R.A. SWEENEY

But for David's sake the LORD his God gave him a lamp in Jerusalem, to raise up his son after him and to establish Jerusalem; because David did what was right in the sight of the LORD, and had not turned aside from anything that He commanded him all the days of his life.

~ 1 KINGS 15:4–5

Asa did what was right in the sight of the LORD , like David his father . . . nevertheless the heart of Asa was wholly devoted to the LORD all his days.

~ 1 KINGS 15:11–14

THE SHOOT OF JESSE

December 16
GOD'S PROPHET

Israel had rebelled against God's kings because the kings were not leading the people into God's kingdom. They set up their own kings, implemented their own gods, and established their own practice of worship. They had turned completely from God and had become pagan idolaters. Their kings were wicked men, and they only became more wicked over time.

A few generations into the line of Israel's kings there arose a king named Ahab. Ahab had married the daughter of a pagan king to form a military alliance, just as Solomon had done, and just as the Torah had instructed the kings not to do. Her name was Jezebel, and she was a cruel and wicked woman who led her husband into all manner of wickedness. Ahab was repeatedly described as being more wicked than any other king.

The wickedness of Ahab and Jezebel was so great that God raised up a special prophet to speak to them: Elijah. God sent Elijah, the prophet, to warn Ahab that, because of his wickedness, God would not send rain in Ahab's kingdom until the people would repent of their idolatry. Elijah then left Ahab's chambers and retreated to the wilderness near a small stream. God provided food for him by sending birds to bring him bread and meat, just as God had miraculously provided food for the Israelites in the wilderness with Moses. After the stream dried up, God sent Elijah to a poor widow in the pagan kingdom to the North. There, God blessed the widow with prosperity and gave her

THE SHOOT OF JESSE

enough to also provide for Elijah as well. God performed several miracles through Elijah during that time, including raising the widow's son to life after the child had suddenly died.

Three and a half years after Elijah had informed Ahab that it would not rain, Elijah returned to Ahab. Jezebel had put all of God's priests in their kingdom to death. The lack of rain was supposed to demonstrate God's power and lead them to repentance, but like Pharaoh, their hearts had become harder, not softer. They blamed God for their troubles.

When Elijah came to Ahab, he told Ahab to summon all the prophets of Ahab's false god to Mount Carmel, along with the people of Israel. They were going to settle, once and for all, who the true god was. When they came to the mountain, the 850 prophets of Ahab's false gods built an extravagant altar and laid a bull to sacrifice on the altar. They spent hours crying out to their false god and performing ceremonies to find favor with their god in hopes that he would send fire from the heavens to consume the offering. Elijah made a humble altar, placed his sacrifice upon it, and drenched the whole thing in water. He prayed a simple prayer for God to make His name known, and God blasted down fire from the heavens that was so intense that it consumed the sacrifice and even the stones too. The people all turned their hearts back to God, and they killed the priests of the false gods. Now that the people had repented, God sent rain for the first time in three and a half years.

Ahab, however, did not repent along with the

people. He returned to his capital city and rallied his army to try to capture Elijah. He didn't dare try to seize him on Mount Carmel because the people had returned to worshiping God and supported Elijah. God gave Elijah strength so that he could outrun Ahab's army, so they never captured him. When Ahab returned with his army, he found war with a neighboring nation and fought against them for years.

There was, at that time, a garden near Ahab's capital city that Ahab really liked. He tried to buy the garden from its owner, but the owner refused. When God had brought the Israelites into the land during Joshua's time, the land had been divided between families so that each family would have their own land forever. It was against the Torah for anyone to sell their family land. The owner of the garden told Ahab that he could not sell him his family land. Ahab became depressed, so Jezebel had the owner murdered and took his garden as a gift for Ahab.

As soon as Jezebel gave the garden to Ahab, God sent Elijah to Ahab. Elijah told Ahab that God was going to bring complete destruction upon Ahab and his family, just as had happened to Ba'asha and Jeroboam. Finally, God's words sunk into Ahab's heart. No one had given themselves to pursue wickedness like Ahab,[10] but at this rebuke from God, Ahab repented from the depths of his heart. He tore his clothes in grief and grieved beyond comfort. God saw that Ahab truly repented and promised to relent of the disaster he planned to bring upon Ahab's household.

Just as Saul was righteous when he had Samuel by his side, Ahab also turned from great evil to righteousness

THE SHOOT OF JESSE

when a righteous prophet was with him. A joint effort between a prophet and a king would be needed to have a righteous kingdom.

> *At the time of the offering of the evening sacrifice, Elijah the prophet came near and said, "O LORD, the God of Abraham, Isaac and Israel, today let it be known that You are God in Israel and that I am Your servant and I have done all these things at Your word. Answer me, O LORD, answer me, that this people may know that You, O LORD, are God, and that You have turned their heart back again." Then the fire of the LORD fell and consumed the burnt offering and the wood and the stones and the dust, and licked up the water that was in the trench. When all the people saw it, they fell on their faces; and they said, 'The LORD, He is God; the LORD, He is God.'*
>
> ~ 1 KINGS 18:36–39

R.A. SWEENEY

Surely there was no one like Ahab who sold himself to do evil in the sight of the Lord, *because Jezebel his wife incited him. He acted very abominably in following idols, according to all that the Amorites had done, whom the* Lord *cast out before the sons of Israel. It came about when Ahab heard these words, that he tore his clothes and put on sackcloth and fasted, and he lay in sackcloth and went about despondently. Then the word of the* Lord *came to Elijah the Tishbite, saying, "Do you see how Ahab has humbled himself before Me? Because he has humbled himself before Me, I will not bring the evil in his days, but I will bring the evil upon his house in his son's days."*

~ 1 Kings 21:25–29

THE SHOOT OF JESSE

December 17
CONSUMED BY FIRE

When the kingdoms separated, Israel's kings were all wicked, and God sent prophets to work to correct the wickedness of the kings. But in Judah, the kings were a mixed bag. Some took after the kings of Israel and led the people of Judah in rebellion. But others were faithful to God to varying degrees and implemented reformations to guide the people in walking with God. God sent prophets to Judah as well. Some were to correct the wicked kings, while others were to guide and encourage the faithful kings. Isaiah was both types of prophets because he lived during the times of both righteous kings and wicked kings of Judah.

Toward the beginning of Isaiah's ministry, he was given a vision. In his vision, he found himself in God's heavenly throne room. There was a train of a robe so large it was almost all that Isaiah could see. As his eyes followed the robe upward, he saw God sitting upon His throne. God was surrounded by flying, flaming serpents that shouted God's praise continually. A voice spoke that shook the foundations of the earth as it rose. Isaiah panicked. He cried out that he would be unmade because he was not holy, but yet was in God's holy presence. Then, one of the flying, fiery serpents took tongs and grabbed a coal from the holy incense fire of God's throne room and came toward Isaiah. Isaiah was doomed.

Isaiah's panic was well-founded. At the garden of Eden, when Adam and Eve sinned, they were exiled from the garden, and the way back was barred by a flaming sword of God's holy presence. God's holiness would incinerate anyone forcing their way into Eden, and Isaiah, who was in Eden in this vision, was a sinner. At Sodom and Gomorrah, God rained down His holiness in the form of fire and obliterated the entire region. When God revealed Himself to the Israelites as they left Egypt He appeared as a pillar of fire and even shielded the Israelites from the Egyptians with His flaming presence. Later, on Mount Sinai, God appeared in fire and terrified the people so much they refused to approach Him out of fear. When Aaron's sons entered the innermost chamber of the tabernacle, where God's presence dwelt, God's holiness, in the form of fire, shot out from the ark and killed them. Elijah called down fire from the heavens on Mount Carmel, and his successor, Elisha, called down fire on soldiers coming to capture him.

God's holiness is not something to be trifled with. If sin were to enter God's presence, it would be incinerated by God's holiness. For Isaiah to find himself in God's throne room, he certainly expected destruction. He must have thought of all the stories of God's presence incinerating the wicked. He must have thought of stories like the death of Uzzah.[11] Then, to see the burning coal coming at him, Isaiah must have been terrified.

The flying serpent brought the coal and touched it to Isaiah. Rather than destroying Isaiah, the serpent proclaimed that Isaiah was now holy, and his sins were forgiven. Isaiah was correct—wickedness cannot endure God's presence. God's holy presence burns away all wickedness and sin. But what Isaiah did not factor in was God's love, mercy, and healing power. Isaiah was a man

R.A. SWEENEY

who desired God's kingdom and repented of his sin when confronted by God's presence. God's holiness did burn away Isaiah's wickedness, but it preserved Isaiah's holy desire for righteousness. Isaiah discovered that God's holiness, while a consuming fire, is not a destroying fire but a purifying one. God's fire burns away the filth so that only that which is pure remains. For those who seek after God and His kingdom, the fire removes that baggage of sin and leaves a purified righteous man or woman. But for those who reject God's kingdom, the fire burns away unrighteousness, only to find there is nothing left.

Sin had been a constant problem for God's kings all the way back to Adam. The Sin Serpent kept enticing God's kings to turn away from God in rebellion and to build the Serpent's kingdom instead of God's. Once the kings had sinned, they were exiled from God because of their wickedness and fled from Him because of their fear. They needed a way back in. Isaiah's vision gave hope. There was a way for humans to be freed from their corruption from sin. There was a way to pass through the fiery sword and enter Eden and God's presence again. The man or woman who approached God in love and repentance could be forgiven. The one who could survive the purifying fire with life to spare could pass through the door into the garden. The one who could lead others through could be the king God wanted.

THE SHOOT OF JESSE

I saw the Lord sitting on a throne, lofty and exalted, with the train of His robe filling the temple. Seraphim stood above Him, each having six wings: with two he covered his face, and with two he covered his feet, and with two he flew. And one called out to another and said,

> *"Holy, Holy, Holy, is the* LORD *of hosts,*
> *The whole earth is full of His glory."* . . .

R.A. SWEENEY

And the foundations of the thresholds trembled at the voice of him who called out, while the temple was filling with smoke. Then I said,

"Woe is me, for I am ruined!
Because I am a man of unclean lips,
And I live among a people of unclean lips;
For my eyes have seen the King, the LORD *of hosts."*

Then one of the seraphim flew to me with a burning coal in his hand, which he had taken from the altar with tongs. He touched my mouth with it and said, "Behold, this has touched your lips; and your iniquity is taken away and your sin is forgiven."

~ ISAIAH 6:1–7

THE SHOOT OF JESSE

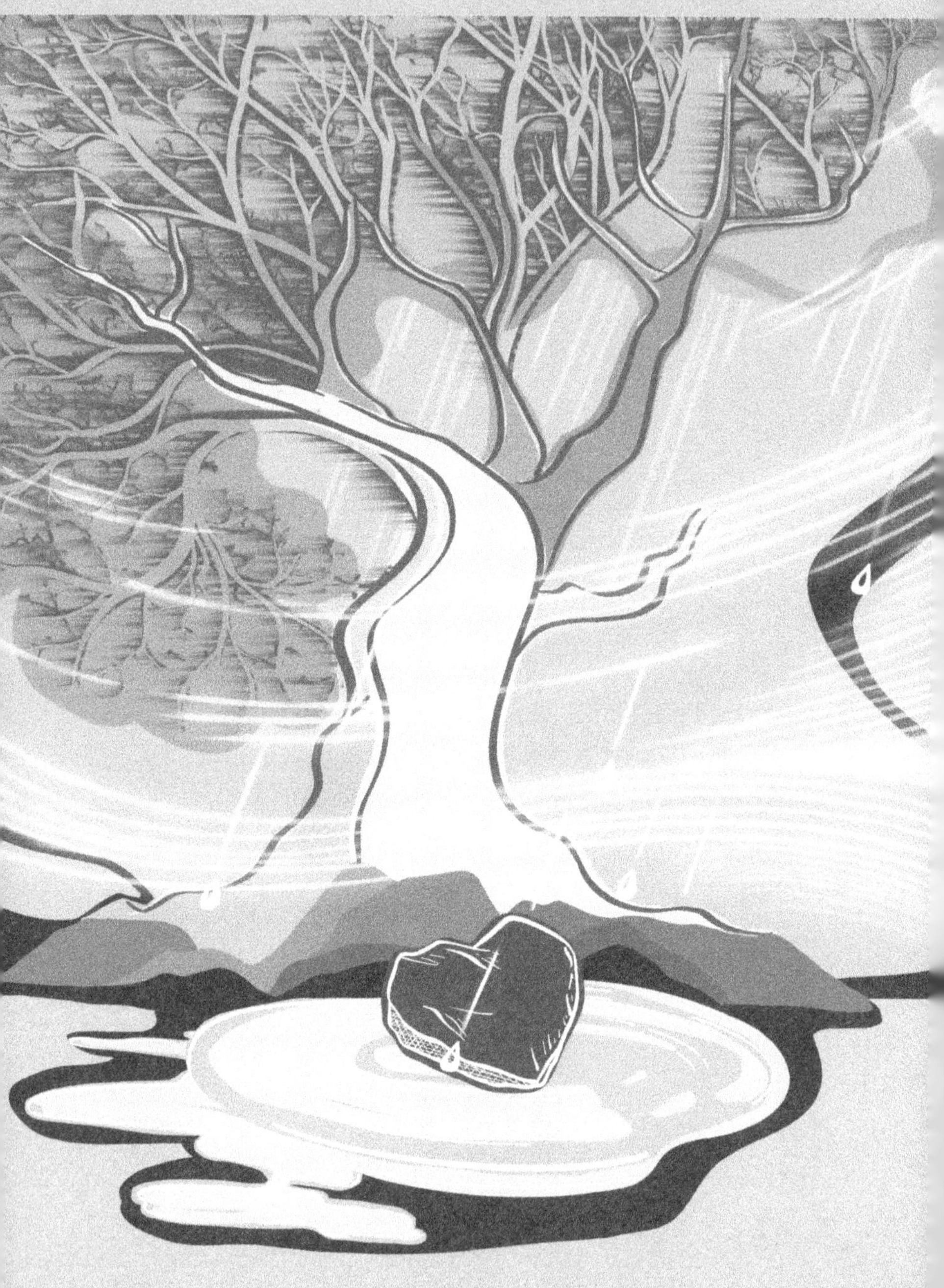

December 18
BACK TO THE WILDERNESS

As the kings of Israel continued to worship idols and reject God, their enemies closed in around them. First, the tribes on the east side of the Jordan River fell to their enemies. Then, slowly but steadily, the power and strength of Israel crumbled until Assyria came and completely destroyed them. Only the nation of Judah was left. But Judah's kings were not much better than Israel's kings. Some were faithful to God, but many were not. They, too, were suffering at the hands of their neighbors, and their kingdom was also crumbling.

During the time that Judah was crumbling, God sent a prophet named Jeremiah to speak to the leaders of Jerusalem and Judah. God's message was that Judah was faithless and treacherous, and that their faithlessness would be their downfall.

Egypt came to Judah during that time and claimed ownership of the nation. The Judaean king was taken prisoner to Egypt, and the pharaoh put a new king on the throne of Judah who would be loyal to him and pay him tribute. This king made secret alliances with Babylon and sold Judah into slavery to Babylon in order to free them from slavery to Egypt.

But the leaders of Judah could not bear the toil of serving Babylon any better than they had with Egypt. They

THE SHOOT OF JESSE

began to plot to rebel against Babylon as well. God spoke through Jeremiah during that time that the people of Judah needed to humble themselves under Babylon. They had made their own mess by being faithless, so God was asking them to demonstrate they could be faithful by remaining loyal to Babylon.

This was too much for the dishonest king, and he rebelled against Babylon as well. Nebuchadnezzar, the king of Babylon, brought an army against Jerusalem and carried the king and all the nobles into exile. Still, Jeremiah spoke God's words to remain faithful to their treaty with Babylon and to seek to bless their oppressor. God told them they would all be taken into exile and that they should embrace the exile, continue to live their lives, and seek the welfare of Babylon. God promised that the exile would be temporary. After a period of seventy years, God would free the people from their exile and bring them home to their land.

But the leaders of Jerusalem continued to rebel against Nebuchadnezzar until, finally, he brought an army to besiege Jerusalem. The siege lasted until the people were starving to death within the city, and finally, the Babylonians broke through the wall. They killed many of those who survived the starvation and carried nearly all the rest of the people off into exile, just as God had spoken through Jeremiah.

This was the final blow against God's people. There was no longer any nation of God's chosen people, only remnants and bands here and there throughout the world. But hope remained. The people clung to the hope spoken through Jeremiah that the exile would only last seventy

R.A. SWEENEY

years. Jeremiah also promised another hope. Ever since Adam, God's people had failed to trust God, walk in His ways, and remain faithful. God spoke through Jeremiah, before the exile, that God would make a new covenant with the people. God was going to write His wisdom into the very hearts of the people so that they would no longer be faithless.

At the same time, a prophet named Ezekiel was speaking God's word to the Judaeans who were already in Babylon. God accused His people of having hard hearts, like Pharaoh from the Exodus story. He promised that He would remove the hard hearts from His people and give them new hearts that could walk in His wisdom. He promised to wash His people clean of the influence of the Sin Serpent and to put His own Spirit within them. All of this, He promised, would make them delight in walking in His wisdom. Because no humans had ever managed to walk faithfully with God, God Himself was going to make a new way for them to be faithful.

At this time, God's people were leaderless. They were scattered across the world. Most were in slavery, poverty, and oppression. They had no home. They had no land. They were broken and destroyed. They were left, in exile, clinging to the promises that God would rescue them and make them into a new kind of humanity. And this new kind of humanity sounded like the type of humans who could reenter Eden.

THE SHOOT OF JESSE

"Behold, days are coming," declares the LORD, *"when I will make a new covenant with the house of Israel and with the house of Judah, not like the covenant which I made with their fathers in the day I took them by the hand to bring them out of the land of Egypt, My covenant which they broke, although I was a husband to them," declares the* LORD. *"But this is the covenant which I will make with the house of Israel after those days," declares the* LORD, *"I will put My law within them and on their heart I will write it; and I will be their God, and they shall be My people. They will not teach again, each man his neighbor and each man his brother, saying, 'Know the* LORD,' *for they will all know Me, from the least of them to the greatest of them," declares the* LORD, *"for I will forgive their iniquity, and their sin I will remember no more."*

~ JEREMIAH 31:31–34

R.A. SWEENEY

I will take you from the nations, gather you from all the lands and bring you into your own land. Then I will sprinkle clean water on you, and you will be clean; I will cleanse you from all your filthiness and from all your idols. Moreover, I will give you a new heart and put a new spirit within you; and I will remove the heart of stone from your flesh and give you a heart of flesh. I will put My Spirit within you and cause you to walk in My statutes, and you will be careful to observe My ordinances. You will live in the land that I gave to your forefathers; so you will be My people, and I will be your God. Moreover, I will save you from all your uncleanness; and I will call for the grain and multiply it, and I will not bring a famine on you.

~ EZEKIEL 36:24–29

THE SHOOT OF JESSE

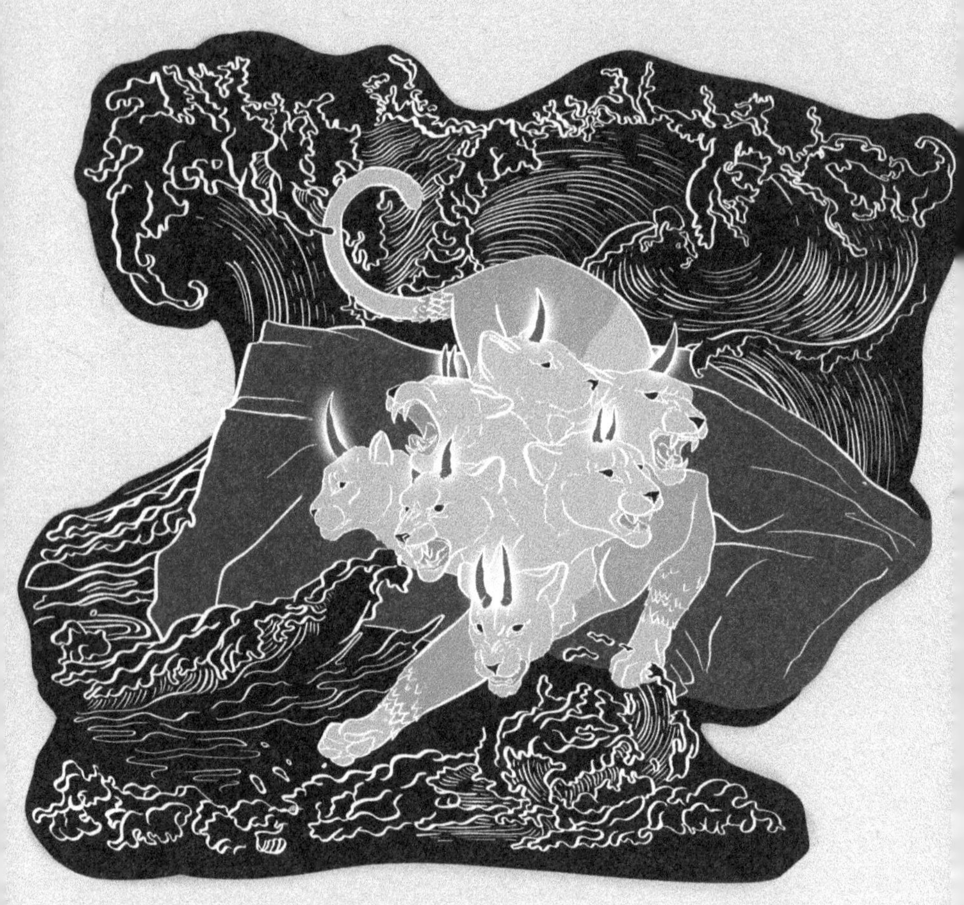

December 19
THE SON OF MAN

When Babylon took control of Jerusalem, they took the nobles of the city and the skilled craftsmen back to Babylon to serve Babylon, and to train them to become Babylonians. This would strengthen the central part of the empire, weaken the conquered people, and reduce the risk of the conquered people groups rebelling against them.

One of the young nobles taken from Judah was a man named Daniel, who was of the royal lineage of Judah. Daniel and three other Jewish young men—Hananiah, Mishael, and Azariah—were taken into the king's special service. The king offered them the best foods in his kingdom, yet they refused and asked to eat only seeds and water. (In Eden, God had assigned seeds for Adam and Eve to eat and provided water for them to drink.) Everyone thought they would starve, but when they lived as though they were in Eden, even while in the very center of Babylon, they thrived and grew strong. This passionate faith and intimacy with God blessed Daniel and his friends.

When the king of Babylon had a nightmare, he became greatly distressed and summoned all his wise men. None of them could help him understand the meaning, just like when Pharaoh had his dream. Just like in Pharaoh's story, only God's servant could interpret the dream, so Daniel came before the king of Babylon and interpreted the dream. The dream the king had seen was that after Babylon's mighty kingdom there would come another kingdom, less glorious than Babylon, and then another less

THE SHOOT OF JESSE

glorious, and another. But eventually, a small kingdom would shatter the existing kingdoms and grow to a massive size, covering the entire world.

The king later set up a massive statue of himself and demanded all the important people in the kingdom to come and worship the statue. Because of their faithfulness to God, Azariah, Hananiah, and Mishael (renamed by the Babylonians as Abed'nego, Shad'rakh, and Meshakh) refused to worship the statue. The king was furious and had them thrown into a blazing hot fire. The king looked into the fire and saw a fourth figure in the flames, whom he described as looking like a "son of the gods."[12] The three Judaeans entered the furnace, but, as Isaiah discovered, the fire only burns away impurity, so the righteous men were unharmed.

Daniel continued to serve the kings. The king of Babylon later had another dream that Daniel interpreted for him. In this dream, God had shown the king that he was like a gigantic tree of life stretching out over the entire world, providing blessings to all the creatures of creation. But in the dream, due to the king's wickedness, his kingdom was taken from him and held for someone else who would be worthy of it. All of this happened like Daniel predicted. And when the next king took the throne and acted even more wickedly, Daniel was the one who came to pronounce judgment against the new king as well.

Eventually, the Persians conquered Babylon, and the Persian king, named Darius, ruled the land. Daniel served Darius as he had served the Babylonian kings. Daniel gained such favor in Darius's eyes that his other officials grew jealous. They trapped Daniel and threw him into a lion's

R.A. SWEENEY

den, but even Darius, the pagan king, prayed to God for Daniel's safety. Daniel spent the night in a walled enclosure (which is what the Hebrew word for "garden" means) at peace with the animals, just as Adam lived in Eden.

During this time, God spoke to Daniel through many of his own visions. The first vision was at the shores of the chaos waters. A gruesome beast, a mutation of the animals of creation, came out of the waters. After that, another mutant beast came out of the waters, followed by a third. The three beasts wreaked havoc on the land. Finally, a fourth beast came out of the chaos waters. This one was more terrifying and destructive than all the others. The fourth beast ravished the entire earth, trampling everyone in its path. Then, God came and set up two thrones. He sat down in judgment, and the beast was condemned and slain. Then, a human called the *Son of Man* was raised from those whom the beast had trampled and brought up upon a cloud (Clouds were a vehicle only God rode upon.) and was seated on the throne next to God. This Son of Man was established as the King of all creation. The beasts in the dream were identified as kingdoms in league with the Sin Serpent. The King who would reenter Eden and rule over all creation as God's steward would be the One who would endure the trampling of the kingdoms of the Sin Serpent and pass through death with life to spare.

The other important vision Daniel received was a visit from the angel, Gabriel. Daniel had held firm to the prophecy from Jeremiah that God would free His people from exile after seventy years. Once the seventy years were completed, by Daniel's calculations, he began praying for

THE SHOOT OF JESSE

God to keep His promise and send the people back to Jerusalem from exile in Babylon. Gabriel appeared and told Daniel he was wrong in two areas. First, it was not seventy years, but seventy Sabbath years, which is 490 years. They still had 420 years to wait. Second, God's promise through Jeremiah was to free the people from a different kind of exile—exile from the garden.

I kept looking in the night visions,
And behold, with the clouds of heaven
One like a Son of Man was coming,
And He came up to the Ancient of Days
And was presented before Him.
And to Him was given dominion,
Glory and a kingdom,
That all the peoples, nations and men of every
language
Might serve Him.
His dominion is an everlasting dominion
Which will not pass away;
And His kingdom is one
Which will not be destroyed.

~ DANIEL 7:13–14

R.A. SWEENEY

Seventy weeks have been decreed for your people and your holy city, to finish the transgression, to make an end of sin, to make atonement for iniquity, to bring in everlasting righteousness, to seal up vision and prophecy and to anoint the most holy place. So you are to know and discern that from the issuing of a decree to restore and rebuild Jerusalem until Messiah the Prince there will be seven weeks and sixty-two weeks; it will be built again, with plaza and moat, even in times of distress.

~ DANIEL 9:24–25

THE SHOOT OF JESSE

December 20
REBUILDING

Way back during Isaiah's time, long before the exile, God spoke through Isaiah that Jerusalem would be destroyed because of the wickedness of the people there. He also promised that He would remake Jerusalem and, in an act of new creation, restore life and beauty to the land. In the middle of this prophecy, God mentioned someone named Cyrus who would fulfill God's purposes by rebuilding Jerusalem and rebuilding the temple.

Generations passed. Jerusalem was destroyed. The people went into exile for decades. First, Babylon ruled them, then the Medes conquered the land. Finally, a Persian king took the throne over that whole region, and his name was Cyrus. Babylon had removed people from their homes and scattered them throughout the empire so they would not unite and rebel. But once Cyrus took the throne, he issued a proclamation throughout his entire empire. He claimed that the Hebrew God had given him the empire and commanded him to allow the Jews to return to their own land to rebuild Jerusalem. He allowed all Jews to return to Jerusalem and commanded all his people to contribute supplies to the rebuilding project. Cyrus was not from the people of Israel, but God spoke to him, and he acknowledged God's words as true.

A Jewish man, named Zerubbabel, the heir to David's line, led the Jews who wished to return on their journey back. He was accompanied by Jeshua, the high priest, and nearly 50,000 people. They took with them all kinds of animals and supplies, and Cyrus gave them all the holy items that had been taken from the temple when Babylon took Jerusalem. Then, they set out for Jerusalem.

When they arrived in the ruins of Jerusalem, they gathered together all those who returned and all the scattered people who were left in the land, built an altar, and the high priest offered sacrifices to God. At that time, one of the holy festivals appointed in the Law was approaching, and the people celebrated the Feast of Booths in compliance with God's instructions. Then, the people began their work and hired craftsmen to begin building.

Once the foundation of the temple was complete, the people came together, and the priest led them in a great celebration in honor of God. Many of the people rejoiced and wept with joy. But many of the older generation lamented and wept in grief, for they knew this was only a shadow of the Solomon's Temple, and they remembered the sorrow of the destruction of Jerusalem.

The neighbors in the land saw the work and the celebration, and they asked to join in to help with the rebuilding in honor of God. The Jews labeled them "enemies" of God's people and refused to allow them to help. These people, offended by the behavior of the Jews, wrote to the king (now a new king) and told him that the Jews were rebuilding in order to rebel. This new king ordered a stop to their work in Jerusalem. During this time, the people gave up any idea of rebuilding the temple but started rebuilding their own houses and businesses instead. It took two prophets speaking the word of God to finally get the people to finish building the temple.

R.A. SWEENEY

Once the temple was finished, the king sent a Jewish scribe named Ezra to Jerusalem to bring sacrifices to God on the king's behalf. Ezra brought the king's sacrifices, and the people also made many sacrifices of their own. Ezra led the people in fasting and praying. He also led them in celebrating the Passover feast again.

After that time, another Jew, Nehemiah, led a third group of people back to Jerusalem. Nehemiah gathered all the people in Jerusalem and led them in rebuilding the wall around Jerusalem. Finally, the kingdom was being built. Ezra brought the people together to read the Law aloud for everyone to hear. Both Ezra and Nehemiah led the people in confessing their sins and promising loyalty to God. Things were looking good for the people living faithfully in the land.

But the leaders of the Jews who led the people back from exile, had been scarred by the destruction of Jerusalem and their time in exile. They remembered the stories of the horror their people faced when Nebuchadnezzar took the city. They had experienced the oppression of exile. They knew that the sins of the people and their continual refusal to obey God's teaching was the cause of all this sorrow. Because of this, they were determined to ensure the people were not faithless again. They began implementing reforms among the people to make them compliant with the teaching that God had given to Moses.

Their biggest focus was on men who had married pagan wives and had kids. Remembering how this corrupted Solomon, the leaders felt this would corrupt the people, so they forced these men to send their pagan wives and their

THE SHOOT OF JESSE

children into the wilderness to die. They also condemned and attacked the practice of slavery. While the American slave trade focused on oppression and demeaning entire people groups, God had actually created a practice of slavery for His people that respected human dignity, was limited in duration, and was an agreed upon relationship. He made this to help those in financial debt work off their debts and have a means of restoration from poverty. God had implemented this practice in order to care for the poor among the Israelites and to give them an opportunity to climb out of poverty. The leaders labeled this practice as unjust and forced people to abandon their responsibility to take the poor under their care for their benefit.

Their zeal for obeying God turned into a legalism that caused them to dishonor God and undermine His plans. The people had begun to rebuild God's kingdom, but their fear and prejudice had laced the foundation of the kingdom with the seeds of its own destruction.

R.A. SWEENEY

*Now when the builders had laid the foundation
of the temple of the LORD, the priests stood in
their apparel with trumpets, and the Levites, the
sons of Asaph, with cymbals, to praise the LORD
according to the directions of King David of
Israel. They sang, praising and giving thanks to
the LORD, saying, "For He is good, for His
lovingkindness is upon Israel forever." And all
the people shouted with a great shout when they
praised the LORD because the foundation of the
house of the LORD was laid. Yet many of the
priests and Levites and heads of fathers'
households, the old men who had seen the first
temple, wept with a loud voice when the
foundation of this house was laid before their
eyes, while many shouted aloud for joy, so that
the people could not distinguish the sound of the
shout of joy from the sound of the weeping of the
people, for the people shouted with a loud shout,
and the sound was heard far away.*

~ EZRA 3:10–13

THE SHOOT OF JESSE

In those days I also saw that the Jews had married women from Ashdod, Ammon and Moab. As for their children, half spoke in the language of Ashdod, and none of them was able to speak the language of Judah, but the language of his own people. So I contended with them and cursed them and struck some of them and pulled out their hair, and made them swear by God, "You shall not give your daughters to their sons, nor take of their daughters for your sons or for yourselves. Did not Solomon king of Israel sin regarding these things? Yet among the many nations there was no king like him, and he was loved by his God, and God made him king over all Israel; nevertheless the foreign women caused even him to sin. Do we then hear about you that you have committed all this great evil by acting unfaithfully against our God by marrying foreign women?" Even one of the sons of Joiada, the son of Eliashib the high priest, was a son-in-law of Sanballat the Horonite, so I drove him away from me. Remember them, O my God, because they have defiled the priesthood and the covenant of the priesthood and the Levites. . . .

R.A. SWEENEY

*Thus I purified them from everything foreign
and appointed duties for the priests and the
Levites, each in his task, and I arranged for the
supply of wood at appointed times and for the
first fruits. Remember me, O my God, for good.*

~ NEHEMIAH 13:23–31

"For I hate divorce," says the LORD, *the God of
Israel, "and him who covers his garment with
wrong," says the* LORD *of hosts. "So take heed to
your spirit, that you do not deal treacherously."*

~ MALACHI 2:16

*For I delight in loyalty rather than sacrifice,
And in the knowledge of God rather than burnt
offerings.*

~ HOSEA 6:6

THE SHOOT OF JESSE

December 21
THE SIGN OF DELIVERANCE

Before Babylon had become a big military power, Aram had been a major power in the North. For a while, Aram had an alliance with the kingdom of Israel (the tribes that had rebelled against God and David's line) in order to fight against Judah and Jerusalem. The people of Judah were terrified, but God spoke through the prophet Isaiah that He was going to protect His chosen people. God would not only prevent Aram and Israel from destroying Judah, but He would also completely wiped-out both Aram and Israel. He was going to bring such destruction on them that they would be blotted out forever.

The people continued to fear and did not trust God's promise, so God offered the people a sign of His power as a demonstration of His ability to rescue His people. The sign God offered was that He would make a virgin give birth to a child. The child would be called *Immanuel* which means "God is with us." Once the people saw this impossible act happen, they would know that God truly was with them and would completely destroy their enemies, who were threatening to wipe them out.

Generations later, God's people were broken. They had rebuilt Jerusalem and the temple after the exile to Babylon, but there was a constant fight between the people who were completely focused on following the rules in God's teaching and those who did not follow God at all.

THE SHOOT OF JESSE

Neither side truly sought to have relationship with God, they only sought to enforce rules or reject Him altogether. Throughout that time, Jerusalem was conquered many times. The Greeks came and conquered the land and defiled the temple. Then the Maccabeus family led a military rebellion against the Greeks and drove them out. Infighting and assassinations, much like Israel had experienced during the time of their kings, left the people weak and ripe for the taking. Finally, the Romans came in and conquered the land. They were cruel oppressors who treated God's people terribly. They were constantly crying out for rescue.

During this time, a young virgin named Mary, descended from David's line, lived in a small backwater town called Nazareth. She was engaged to a man but not yet married. One day, the angel Gabriel appeared to her. He greeted her by calling her a woman of favor, a title derived from the Proverbs for a woman who lives by God's wisdom. He told her she would give birth to a Son while still a virgin and that her Son would become the new King of God's people forever. After asking some questions, Mary praised God and rejoiced that God had given her such blessing.

Gabriel also visited the man Mary was engaged to, Joseph. He was described as a righteous man and also from the line of David. Once Gabriel identified himself, Joseph (because only males were taught the Scriptures) must have thought of the book of Daniel, the only place Gabriel was named in the Scriptures of the Jews. This would have brought ideas of the Son of Man figure being trampled by the beast and ascending to the heavenly throne on a cloud and of the promise of release from exile after 490 years. (That promise would have been made about 460 years before Gabriel visited Joseph.) Gabriel also quoted from the book of Isaiah to explain Mary's virgin pregnancy. Joseph must have known that a virgin birth was a sign of a coming defeat of the enemies of God's people and rescue from oppression for the people. All signs pointed to God preparing to defeat the Romans and rescue His people to be a free nation once again.

But Gabriel also mentioned one other thing to Joseph. The Son that would come from this virgin birth was to be named Yeshua, which is Hebrew for "God sets free." Gabriel said that this would be the Child's name because He would free His people *from their sins*. This was a strange and unexpected turn of events. Certainly, many recognized that the Roman occupation of their land was caused by the failure of the people to obey God. But to call removing Roman occupation from their land "freeing them from their sins" was an odd thing to say. Or did freeing them from their sins mean something else?

They were left to wonder, what did all this mean? Certainly, God was going to rescue the people. It was clear God was going to destroy their enemies. But how did the beast trampling the Son of Man fit in? How was God going to free them from exile when they were living in their own land? Exile wasn't the problem, military occupation and oppression were. And how did this all tie into liberation from sin? The picture all this painted remained blurry.

THE SHOOT OF JESSE

Then the LORD *spoke again to Ahaz, saying, "Ask a sign for yourself from the* LORD *your God; make it deep as Sheol or high as heaven." But Ahaz said, "I will not ask, nor will I test the* LORD*!" Then he said, "Listen now, O house of David! Is it too slight a thing for you to try the patience of men, that you will try the patience of my God as well? Therefore the* LORD *Himself will give you a sign: Behold, a virgin will be with child and bear a son, and she will call His name Immanuel. He will eat curds and honey at the time He knows enough to refuse evil and choose good. For before the boy will know enough to refuse evil and choose good, the land whose two kings you dread will be forsaken.*

~ ISAIAH 7:10–16

Now in the sixth month the angel Gabriel was sent from God to a city in Galilee called Nazareth, to a virgin engaged to a man whose name was Joseph, of the descendants of David; and the virgin's name was Mary. And coming in, he said to her, "Greetings, favored one! The Lord is with you." But she was very perplexed at this statement, and kept pondering what kind of . . .

R.A. SWEENEY

salutation this was. The angel said to her, "Do not be afraid, Mary; for you have found favor with God. And behold, you will conceive in your womb and bear a son, and you shall name Him Jesus. He will be great and will be called the Son of the Most High; and the Lord God will give Him the throne of His father David; and He will reign over the house of Jacob forever, and His kingdom will have no end."

~ LUKE 1:26–33

But when he had considered this, behold, an angel of the Lord appeared to him in a dream, saying, "Joseph, son of David, do not be afraid to take Mary as your wife; for the Child who has been conceived in her is of the Holy Spirit. She will bear a Son; and you shall call His name Jesus, for He will save His people from their sins." Now all this took place to fulfill what was spoken by the Lord through the prophet: "BEHOLD, THE VIRGIN SHALL BE WITH CHILD AND SHALL BEAR A SON, AND THEY SHALL CALL HIS NAME IMMANUEL," which translated means, "GOD WITH US."

~ MATTHEW 1:20–23

THE SHOOT OF JESSE

December 22
THE BUDDING OF A KINGDOM

When it was nearly time for the baby to be born, the Roman emperor called for a census of his entire kingdom. This meant that everyone in the empire was to return to the city of their ancestors to be counted. Joseph and Mary packed up and made the trip to Bethlehem. This was Joseph's ancestral home because he was descended from David, who came from Bethlehem. But this was no longer a place where David's family would be honored. They found no room at any house of lodging and were forced to live in a shelter for animals.

While there, Mary gave birth to a Son. But this Child, who was foretold would be a King, did not get a king's reception. In place of a royal nursery, this Child was placed in a feed trough for the animals. Angels appeared that night in a field where shepherds were tending their flocks. They were told the *good news* of the birth of a savior and rushed to find Mary, Joseph, and the Child. The King did not have important guests coming to Him at His birth. Instead, He was surrounded by beasts and greeted by lowly social outcasts. This was who the King had come for—the lowly and the outcasts. On the eighth day, as was Jewish custom, the family went to Jerusalem, offered the appropriate sacrifices, and named the boy Yeshua (which we translate as Jesus).

THE SHOOT OF JESSE

Many months later, a group of Eastern scholars arrived in Jerusalem. They went to King Herod to ask where the Child, who was the new King of the Jews, had been born. They had come for many hundreds of miles to worship this King and bring Him gifts. This caused an uproar throughout all of Jerusalem. Herod and his supporters were upset because Herod was the king of the Jews. Others were hopeful that a new king would mean better lives. Still others were hopeful that this new king could be the promised King and Messiah of the Jews. The whole region was abuzz.

Herod consulted with his Scripture scholars and determined that the Child would have been born in Bethlehem. Herod sent the Eastern scholars on their way to Bethlehem, asking that they return once they found the Child to tell Herod where to find the boy, saying that he, too, wanted to go worship the new King.

The Eastern scholars came to Bethlehem, guided by a star. They entered the house they were led to and found Mary and her Son. They bowed down in worship and presented gifts. Some of the scholars brought gifts of gold. This was a present typically reserved for kings. By giving Jesus this gift, they honored Him as a King. Other scholars presented gifts of frankincense. This was what priests would burn in the temple before God as a means of bringing the thanks and prayers of the people before God. By giving Jesus this, they were acknowledging His role as God's Priest and giving Him the tools they assumed a priest would need. The remaining scholars brought gifts of myrrh. This was a perfume used by the wealthy for multiple purposes. Almost

R.A. SWEENEY

every time myrrh was mentioned in the Scriptures, it was used by brides and grooms to anoint themselves before coming together in marriage. All throughout the writings of the prophets, God described the day when He would come and rescue creation from the Sin Serpent and would be united with His people, just like a husband uniting with his wife. This process was often described by the prophets using wedding and marriage language. These scholars were giving Jesus a gift to prepare Him for His marriage to His people.

The scholars stayed in Bethlehem for a while and honored Jesus and His family. When it was time for them to leave, God gave them visions and dreams. In them, God warned the scholars not to return through Jerusalem because Herod was planning to kill Jesus. So, the scholars left Bethlehem and returned home by a different way.

Once Herod found out the Eastern scholars had betrayed him, he was enraged. Herod recognized that a new king, whether he was the Messiah or not, was a threat to him and his power. He wanted this new King out of the picture. Immediately, Herod mobilized his personal guard and sent them to Bethlehem to kill Jesus. Since they could not be sure which child was Jesus, their instructions were to kill every male child around the age they calculated that Jesus would have been. But before Herod's men could get there, God warned Joseph in a dream to flee from Bethlehem down to Egypt. They were gone by the time Herod's men got to Bethlehem, but the guard still slaughtered every boy that was two years old or younger.

Joseph, Mary, and Jesus lived in Egypt until Herod

THE SHOOT OF JESSE

died. Then God told them to return. They came back only to find Herod's son in charge, so they moved back to Nazareth, which was a small town in the middle of nowhere. They were safe in this tiny village, and Jesus grew into a man.

As soon as He was born, Jesus began attracting those who would be a part of His kingdom, but He also was immediately attacked by those who did not want to see His kingdom established on earth.

Now after Jesus was born in Bethlehem of Judea in the days of Herod the king, magi from the east arrived in Jerusalem, saying, "Where is He who has been born King of the Jews? For we saw His star in the east and have come to worship Him." When Herod the king heard this, he was troubled, and all Jerusalem with him. Gathering together all the chief priests and scribes of the people, he inquired of them where the Messiah was to be born.

~ MATTHEW 2:1–5

R.A. SWEENEY

Now when they had gone, behold, an angel of the Lord appeared to Joseph in a dream and said, "Get up! Take the Child and His mother and flee to Egypt, and remain there until I tell you; for Herod is going to search for the Child to destroy Him." So Joseph got up and took the Child and His mother while it was still night, and left for Egypt. He remained there until the death of Herod. This was to fulfill what had been spoken by the Lord through the prophet: "OUT OF EGYPT I CALLED MY SON."

~ MATTHEW 2:13–15

And Jesus kept increasing in wisdom and stature, and in favor with God and men.

~ LUKE 2:52

THE SHOOT OF JESSE

December 23
HAS THE KINGDOM COME?

Jesus grew into a man among the Jewish people in Galilee, the small and poor region to the north of Jerusalem. As He grew into manhood, He began teaching people about God and about the kingdom God wanted to bring on the earth. As He taught, He began to gather a large following. Eventually, He gathered twelve men who faithfully followed Him wherever the ministry took Him. There were also many women who followed Jesus around and others who were not part of His twelve disciples. As He traveled, He performed all kinds of miracles to show love and mercy to the poor and broken people He met.

In addition to those who followed Him, Jesus also planted communities all over the region, consisting of people who were seeking after the kingdom He taught about. Some people were allowed to join Him as He traveled around, but He instructed others to stay put so that they could share the good news of this kingdom with all the people in their communities.

One of the earliest people to hope for this kingdom and proclaim it openly was a man named John. He was called the *Baptizer* because when people came to hear him preach about the kingdom, he encouraged them to engage in a ritual washing called *baptism*. Baptism was a symbol of the sinful flesh entering into the waters of death, only to pass through into a new kind of life. John was a strange man

THE SHOOT OF JESSE

who attracted many people to hear his preaching, but he always pointed to his hope in the Messiah. Jesus even came to John to be baptized to signal the beginning of His ministry of leading people into death and out the other side. When Jesus came, John announced to the whole crowd that Jesus was the Messiah he was hoping in.

But, as Jesus began His mission, it didn't look like what John thought the Messiah's mission would be. John expected a revolutionary, who would unite the faithful to fight off the wicked and create a kingdom of purity. But from what he heard, Jesus's ministry was mostly teaching about showing love to others and healing people. John did not understand how this could be the work of the Messiah he had waited so long for. He began to doubt.

In his doubt, John sent some of those who helped in his ministry to go to Jesus. John had them ask about his doubts. He had expected a very different Messiah. They asked Jesus if He was, in fact, the Messiah that John thought He was, or if someone else was to come. Jesus instructed these men to watch as He healed many of the sick and broken people who were coming to Him. Then He told them to return to John and tell him what they had seen—

> *"The BLIND RECEIVE SIGHT, the lame walk, the lepers are cleansed, and the deaf hear, the dead are raised up, and the poor HAVE THE GOSPEL PREACHED TO THEM. Blessed is he who does not take offense at Me."* [13]

These were quotes from and allusions to a few prophecies of Isaiah. In one, from Isaiah 35, God spoke of the coming kingdom. The coming of the kingdom looked like a new act of creation like we saw in Genesis 2. The dry ground became watered. Plants sprang up. There was abundance and prosperity. Every manner of illness, brokenness, and deformity would be healed, and all humans would be restored to the picture of how God intended them to be. Then, all humanity would come to their God to receive the reward for their behavior. Those who desired God would receive reward, while those who rejected God would be sent into exile.

The other prophecy was from Isaiah 61. Jesus actually quoted this passage at another time to kick off His ministry. This was the mission statement of His work that He proclaimed as He began. This prophecy pointed to the coming of the Messiah in a similar way but also a little differently. Rather than describing a new act of creation after the fashion of Genesis 2, this depicted the coming of the Messiah as a great wedding party. The sick and broken were healed as gifts from the Groom to those who came to His wedding. There would be restoration and abundance as the Groom lavishly spared no expense to celebrate the union between Him and His beloved bride. But the bride and the guests become mixed into a single entity in the prophecy as the invited guests were also the bride herself. The people would be joined to God as a bride to her husband and would be invited to join in the celebration and love of the wedding. And, of course, the wedding and celebration take place in a beautiful garden.

This was Jesus's answer to John's questions and doubts. Jesus sent back the evidence of His works, as seen by John's followers, and told John to decide for himself if

THE SHOOT OF JESSE

this was what the kingdom would look like. There was also an implied question—if this wasn't the coming of the kingdom, what else could the kingdom coming look like?

143

R.A. SWEENEY

When the men came to Him, they said, "John the Baptist has sent us to You, to ask, 'Are You the Expected One, or do we look for someone else?'" At that very time He cured many people of diseases and afflictions and evil spirits; and He gave sight to many who were blind. And He answered and said to them, "Go and report to John what you have seen and heard: the BLIND RECEIVE SIGHT, *the lame walk, the lepers are cleansed, and the deaf hear, the dead are raised up, the* POOR HAVE THE GOSPEL PREACHED TO THEM. *Blessed is he who does not take offense at Me."*

~ Luke 7:20–23

THE SHOOT OF JESSE

Say to those with anxious heart,
"Take courage, fear not.
Behold, your God will come with vengeance;
The recompense of God will come,
But He will save you."
Then the eyes of the blind will be opened
And the ears of the deaf will be unstopped.
Then the lame will leap like a deer,
And the tongue of the mute will shout for joy.
For waters will break forth in the wilderness
And streams in the Arabah.
The scorched land will become a pool
And the thirsty ground springs of water;
In the haunt of jackals, its resting place,
Grass becomes reeds and rushes.

~ ISAIAH 35:4–7

R.A. SWEENEY

The Spirit of the Lord GOD is upon me,
Because the LORD has anointed me
To bring good news to the afflicted;
He has sent me to bind up the brokenhearted,
To proclaim liberty to captives
And freedom to prisoners;
To proclaim the favorable year of the LORD
And the day of vengeance of our God;
To comfort all who mourn,
To grant those who mourn in Zion,
Giving them a garland instead of ashes,
The oil of gladness instead of mourning,
The mantle of praise instead of a spirit of
fainting.
So they will be called oaks of righteousness,
The planting of the LORD, that He may be
glorified.

~ ISAIAH 61:1–3

THE SHOOT OF JESSE

December 24
TRAMPLED BY THE BEAST

Jesus continued His ministry for about three years. He traveled all over the land of Israel teaching and healing so that all the poor and broken could see, hear, or experience little bits of the kingdom Jesus was bringing. But Jesus also extended His demonstrations of God's love to people the Jews considered their enemies. He even invited those people to enter into God's kingdom along with the Jewish people. This upset many of the Jews.

At that time, there was a group of Jewish religious leaders called *Pharisees*. These Pharisees followed after Ezra's example—practicing a strict compliance to God's Torah based on their interpretations and demanding others do the same. Like Ezra, the practice of their faith was largely characterized by following traditions more than developing relationships with God. Jesus demonstrated God's love to them by telling them they were not right with God and that they needed to repent. This upset the Pharisees, and they had a lot of power and influence in that land.

Eventually, Jesus's love for people had upset enough people that they decided to act against Him. The Jewish leaders arrested Jesus and turned Him over to the Romans to be executed. The Roman governor of that region was named Pontius Pilate. He questioned Jesus and found no fault in Him. But Jesus also did not offer any defense against

THE SHOOT OF JESSE

the accusations brought against Him. He simply said that this was part of God's plan and that He was entering into death willingly.

Pilate summoned the Jewish people to come before him. Once there, Pilate brought out two men before the crowd. The first man was Jesus of Nazareth, called *King of the Jews*. The other man was named Jesus *Barabbas*, which means "Son of our Fathers." Pilate agreed to release one of them and put the other to death, and he allowed the Jews to decide which Jesus would receive which fate. They could receive back Jesus, the son of their fathers, a violent man accused of rebelling against Rome and killing people, or they could receive back Jesus of Nazareth. This Jesus very conspicuously did not have His Father named in the charges, as if to call attention to the need for the crowd to decide if He really was the Son of God. Pilate even confessed to the crowd that he had found no guilt in this Jesus of Nazareth.

The Jewish leaders stirred up the crowd to demand Barabbas be released and Jesus of Nazareth be put to death. Pilate tried to change their minds, but the Jewish leaders continued to stir up the crowd to kill Jesus of Nazareth. Even the people who had celebrated the marvelous works of Jesus of Nazareth were now part of the corrupt actions of wicked men, working to kill Him. Pilate finally agreed, released Barabbas, and sent Jesus of Nazareth to be executed.

Once Pilate had turned Jesus over to the guards, they began to abuse Him. They took thorny branches, wove them into a crown, and beat it into His head. They dressed

R.A. SWEENEY

Jesus in royal purple robes, gave Him a staff made of reeds, and bowed down, as if worshiping Jesus, all as ways of mocking Him. They tied Him to a post and whipped Him until all the flesh on His back had been stripped off.

Once the guards grew tired of humiliating and abusing Jesus, they loaded a large wooden cross onto His fleshless back. They forced Him to carry the cross through the streets on the way up to a mountain called *The Skull*. Once at The Skull, they laid Jesus on the cross and drove large metal spikes through His wrists and ankles into the cross. They stood the cross up, so He hung upon the cross in the air. If He relaxed His muscles, He would slide down the rough wooden cross a little and would be unable to breathe. If He wanted to breathe, He needed to pull against the nails in His wrists and push against the nails in His ankles to slide His shredded back upward against the wood so He could gasp for breath. In exhaustion, He would slide His shredded back down the wood. And when He was nearly suffocated, He would slide it back up by the nails in His bones. They also hung a sign above Him that said "King of the Jews."

While this was happening, He continued to show love to those around Him and to forgive those who repented of mocking and crucifying Him. All the while, people came by to mock Him and ridicule Him. He continued using the little strength and breath He had to love and bless others until He finally died. To check that He was dead, they stabbed His side with a spear, and water and blood poured out. Then some followers of Jesus took His body and laid it in a tomb. Jesus had descended into death.

THE SHOOT OF JESSE

The crowds, the Jewish leaders, and the Romans had become the beast that trampled the Son of Man to death.

But Jesus kept silent. And the high priest said to Him, "I adjure You by the living God, that You tell us whether You are the Christ, the Son of God." Jesus said to him, "You have said it yourself; nevertheless I tell you, hereafter you will see the SON OF MAN SITTING AT THE RIGHT HAND OF POWER, and COMING ON THE CLOUDS OF HEAVEN." Then the high priest tore his robes and said, "He has blasphemed! What further need do we have of witnesses? Behold, you have now heard the blasphemy; what do you think?" They answered, "He deserves death!" Then they spat in His face and beat Him with their fists; and others slapped Him.

~ MATTHEW 26:63–67

R.A. SWEENEY

Therefore Pilate entered again into the Praetorium, and summoned Jesus and said to Him, "Are You the King of the Jews?" Jesus answered, "Are you saying this on your own initiative, or did others tell you about Me?" Pilate answered, "I am not a Jew, am I? Your own nation and the chief priests delivered You to me; what have You done?" Jesus answered, "My kingdom is not of this world. If My kingdom were of this world, then My servants would be fighting so that I would not be handed over to the Jews; but as it is, My kingdom is not of this realm." Therefore Pilate said to Him, "So You are a king?" Jesus answered, "You say correctly that I am a king. For this I have been born, and for this I have come into the world, to testify to the truth. Everyone who is of the truth hears My voice."

~ JOHN 18:33–37

THE SHOOT OF JESSE

*When they came to the place called The Skull,
there they crucified Him and the criminals, one
on the right and the other on the left. But Jesus
was saying, "Father, forgive them; for they do not
know what they are doing." And they cast lots,
dividing up His garments among themselves.
And the people stood by, looking on. And even the
rulers were sneering at Him, saying, "He saved
others; let Him save Himself if this is the Christ
of God, His Chosen One." The soldiers also
mocked Him, coming up to Him, offering Him
sour wine, and saying, "If You are the King of the
Jews, save Yourself!" Now there was also an
inscription above Him, "THIS IS THE KING OF
THE JEWS." One of the criminals who were
hanged there was hurling abuse at Him, saying,
"Are You not the Christ? . . .*

R.A. SWEENEY

Save Yourself and us!" But the other answered, and rebuking him said, "Do you not even fear God, since you are under the same sentence of condemnation? And we indeed are suffering justly, for we are receiving what we deserve for our deeds; but this man has done nothing wrong." And he was saying, "Jesus, remember me when You come in Your kingdom!" And He said to him, "Truly I say to you, today you shall be with Me in Paradise."

~ LUKE 23:33–43

THE SHOOT OF JESSE

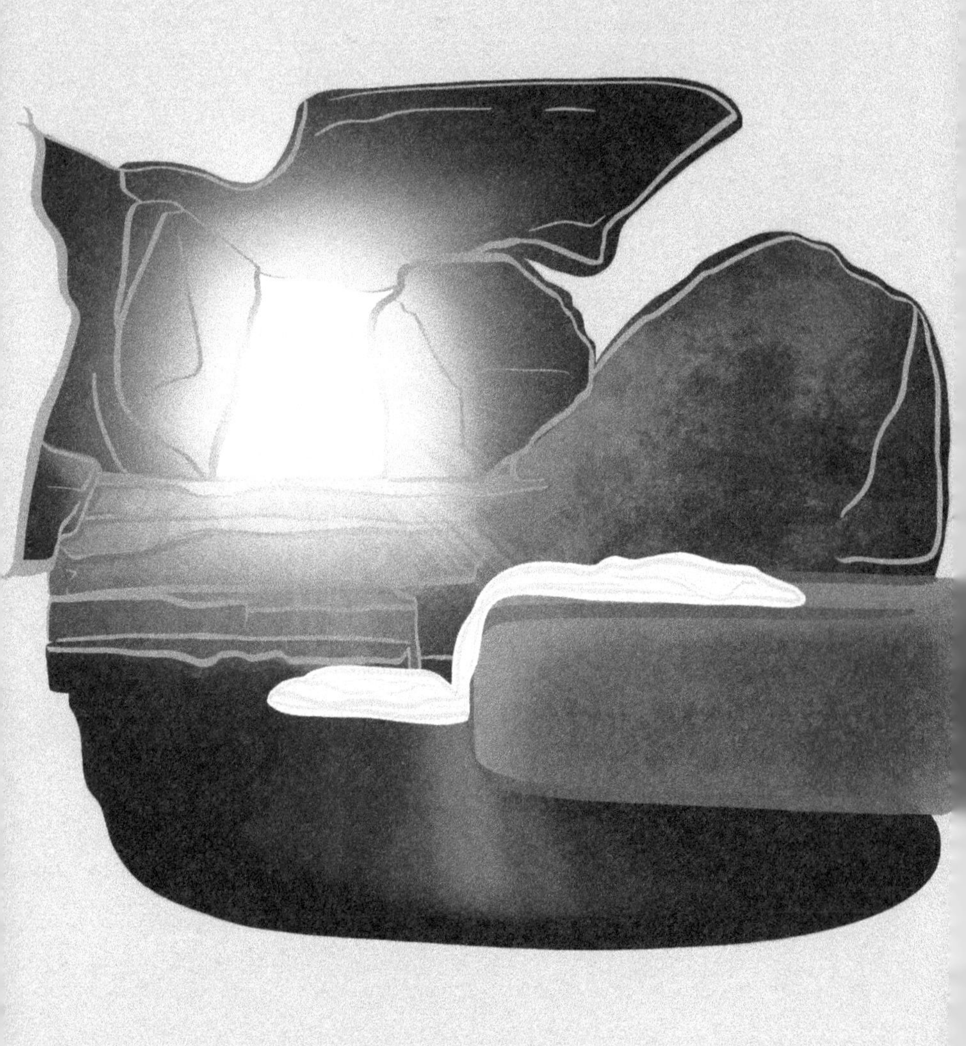

December 25
OUT THE OTHER SIDE

Jesus had died. He was placed in a tomb, the very act of the grave swallowing Him up. Rome, who had devoured all the nations of the world, had conspired with God's chosen people. Together, this mutant hybrid of God's people and the beastly devourer of nations trampled Jesus and drove His broken body into the dust. They thought they had beaten Him. The Sin Serpent's kingdom had struck Jesus with a fatal blow.

But then, Sunday morning came. The women who had followed Jesus during His life came to the tomb to put oils and perfumes on Him as a final blessing. Though, when they arrived the stone door of the tomb was already removed from the mouth of the cave. They peered in and found Jesus was gone.

They had not understood that this was all God's plan. They did not know that the crown of thorns beaten into Jesus's head was actually His coronation ceremony. They did not know that, when the guards dressed Him in purple and gave Him a reed staff, He was actually being clothed in His royal garb. They did not know that the guards mocking Him were actually the first ones to bow before the new King of all creation. They did not know that, when Jesus was paraded through the streets, it was actually the celebration of His ascension to the Kingship. They did not

THE SHOOT OF JESSE

know that, when He was raised into the air on the cross, this was actually the way in which King Jesus would be made "high and lifted up"[14] for the nations to see. And when Pilate had the inscription "King of the Jews" posted above Jesus's head in multiple languages, he made the proclamation to every people and tongue[15] that this truly was the new King.

Jesus's first act as the King of creation, who reigns in obedience to God, was to faithfully enter into death. God's ultimate test to demonstrate whether a human is ready to receive the blessings of Eden is for the human to enter into death faithfully, trusting that God's power is greater even than death. This was Noah's test as he entered the waters of death. This was Abraham's test as he was told to give up any hope of a lineage with Isaac. This was Judah's test when he offered himself to Egyptian imprisonment. This was the Israelites' test as they were told to trust the Passover lamb and to cross through the waters of death. Again and again, God would test His people in this way and would reward those who trusted Him. Jesus had passed this test when He willingly went to the cross and remained there until His death. And, as always, God proved trustworthy in His commitment to Jesus and proved powerful in His confrontation with death.

Jesus wasn't brought back from death, as many others had been. He was brought through death and out the other side into a newness of life. He wasn't returned to His state of mortality, destined to suffer the weakness of flesh and the pain of death once again. Instead, Jesus was born into a new kind of life, an immortal kind of life. This kind of

R.A. SWEENEY

life is still lived in fleshly bodies, but bodies that are not corrupted by sin, death, and violence.

The grave proved to be the flaming sword in the Garden of Eden. Jesus had passed through the fire, entering with faith in a God more powerful than death and able to rescue from the fire. Like Daniel's friends, Jesus found God was with Him through the fiery ordeal. Like Isaiah, Jesus found God's purifying fire of testing only destroys that which is wicked and has no power to destroy that which is righteous. Like Daniel saw in his vision, Jesus was able to become King of the universe by allowing the beast to trample Him to death. As God told Adam and Eve, Jesus was the promised Seed of the woman who would suffer the worst the Sin Serpent could throw His way but would ultimately destroy the power of the Serpent in the process. And just as Daniel saw in his vision, when Jesus's time on earth was ended, He was carried into the heavens upon a cloud to be seated on the throne at God's right hand.

At last, the curse had been reversed. The Sin Serpent had been crushed. There was a Human able to enter back into Eden. He was the King, like David, in harmony with a Priest, like Samuel, and with a Prophet, like Elijah. There was a Royal Priest in Eden, overseeing all creation to restore God's original work to a perfected ideal. There was a Faithful Steward in the garden to heal and correct all the brokenness and disorder in creation. There was One with life in such abundance that He could enter death and come out the other side with life to spare. There was a Trustworthy Guide to lead His people through the fiery sword so that they, too, might experience Eden's blessing

THE SHOOT OF JESSE

and God's abundance. And just as the water of life came forth from the tree of life in the garden of Eden, so too water had poured from Jesus, nailed to a tree. He was now the Tree of Life that poured forth the blessing and abundance of God's love to the world.

The story of the Bible tells of God creating a perfect blank canvas for humans to spend an eternity with God shaping the canvas into a masterpiece. Once humanity forfeited that calling and were exiled from the garden, the rest of the story is a search for the One to lead us back to the garden. Jesus is that One, and He succeeded where everyone else had failed. We can come to Him, and He will welcome us back into the garden. He will wash us clean. He will replace our hard hearts. He will fill us with His Spirit. He will write God's word on our hearts. He will guide us through the fiery sword. He will provide us with life enough to pass through death with life to spare. Praise be to God for His faithful love to rescue us at immeasurable cost!

R.A. SWEENEY

But on the first day of the week, at early dawn, they came to the tomb bringing the spices which they had prepared. And they found the stone rolled away from the tomb, but when they entered, they did not find the body of the Lord Jesus. While they were perplexed about this, behold, two men suddenly stood near them in dazzling clothing; and as the women were terrified and bowed their faces to the ground, the men said to them, "Why do you seek the living One among the dead? He is not here, but He has risen. Remember how He spoke to you while He was still in Galilee, saying that the Son of Man must be delivered into the hands of sinful men, and be crucified, and the third day rise again."

~ LUKE 24:1–7

THE SHOOT OF JESSE

Now He said to them, "These are My words which I spoke to you while I was still with you, that all things which are written about Me in the Law of Moses and the Prophets and the Psalms must be fulfilled." Then He opened their minds to understand the Scriptures, and He said to them, "Thus it is written, that the Christ would suffer and rise again from the dead the third day, and that repentance for forgiveness of sins would be proclaimed in His name to all the nations, beginning from Jerusalem. You are witnesses of these things. And behold, I am sending forth the promise of My Father upon you; but you are to stay in the city until you are clothed with power from on high." And He led them out as far as Bethany, and He lifted up His hands and blessed them. While He was blessing them, He parted from them and was carried up into heaven.

~ LUKE 24:44–51

R.A. SWEENEY

Then he showed me a river of the water of life, clear as crystal, coming from the throne of God and of the Lamb, in the middle of its street. On either side of the river was the tree of life, bearing twelve kinds of fruit, yielding its fruit every month; and the leaves of the tree were for the healing of the nations. There will no longer be any curse; and the throne of God and of the Lamb will be in it, and His bond-servants will serve Him; they will see His face, and His name will be on their foreheads. And there will no longer be any night; and they will not have need of the light of a lamp nor the light of the sun, because the Lord God will illumine them; and they will reign forever and ever. And he said to me, "These words are faithful and true"; and the Lord, the God of the spirits of the prophets, sent His angel to show to His bondservants the things which must soon take place. And behold, I am coming quickly. Blessed is he who heeds the words of the prophecy of this book."

~ REVELATION 22:1–7

THE SHOOT OF JESSE

R.A. SWEENEY

Endnotes

1 Genesis 1:1

2 Peter Jackson, dir. *The Hobbit: An Unexpected Journey.*
    2012; Burbank, CA: New Line Cinema and MGM
    Studios, 2012. Blu-ray Disc, 1080p HD.

3 Genesis 1:2 Author's translation

4 Genesis 15:6

5 Hebrews 11:18-19

6 Judges 21:25

7 1 Samuel 3:10

8 1 Kings 10:27

9 1 Kings 4:25

10 1 Kings 21:25

11 2 Samuel 6

12 Daniel 3:25

13 Luke 7:22–23

14 Isaiah 6:1; 52:13

15 Isaiah 2:2-3

www.ingramcontent.com/pod-product-compliance
Lightning Source LLC
Chambersburg PA
CBHW040141160726
48006CB00014B/1580